SOYINKA'S METAMORPHOSIS

SOYINKA'S
METAMORPHOSIS
ECHOES FROM "THE PEOPLE'S MANDATE"

SUNNY IGBOANUGO

FOREWORD

Professor Wole Soyinka, Africa's first Nobel laureate in Literature, is a celebrated Poet, Novelist, Essayist and Playwright, who has devoted the greater part of his life in the fight against corruption, bad governance and injustice, wherever he finds one. He once admonished the youths," Only in Africa will thieves be regrouping to loot again and the youths whose future is being stolen will be celebrating it ...."

To many observers, the Nobel laureate has since moved from his original position to a new but strange status, that millions of Nigerians are struggling to comprehend. It is like moving from the penthouse to the basement, in what is interpreted in some quarters as see-evil-keep-mum attitude, which has seemingly progressed since 2015, in the years of President Muhammadu Buhari and may have reached the anti-climax.

So, when Sunny Igboanugo, a veteran journalist observed these contradictions, using Soyinka's engagements over the 2023 presidential election in Nigeria, particularly as it relates to Peter Obi, the Presidential Candidate of Labour Party (LP), the erudite scholar and celebrated playwright seemed to have been so angered that he reached for his pen once again, to author in his "Intervention XII, BAITING IGBOPHOBIA: The Sunny Igboanugo Thesis", a push back. The content of the intervention showed how deeply the sage was touched by Igboanugo's position.

In return, however, the veteran journalist seems not to have succumbed to silence by the powerful influence and cryptic expressions of the sage but instead attempted to give his response in his well-researched and highly detailed work. This is an engaging piece.

Ben Benson-Okoli Esq.

ABOUT THE AUTHOR

Soyinka's Metamorphosis: Echoes from "The Stolen Mandate" is written to protest the new trend in Nigeria by certain interests to target the Igbo through ethnic labelling. It is to draw global attention to the danger of taking away The Nigerian Identity from Ndigbo and forcing them into an ethnic straightjacket to achieve a predetermined purpose. It is a protest against forcing them never to speak as Nigerians but as The Igbo.

Sunny Igboanugo, a graduate of Mass Communication, is a veteran journalist of more than three decades standing. His career began in The Guardian in 1991. He was posted to Delta State as the first correspondent at the creation of the state in 1991 and later Enugu, where he spent a decade in the same capacity, before joining Daily Independent as a pioneer staff in 2001 as Enugu Bureau Chief. Another stint there saw him rise in different capacities including Group Politics Editor and finally Deputy Chairman of the Editorial Board before he left in 2013. He is currently the Publisher of *Whirlwindnews.com.ng*, an online newspaper in Nigeria.

During his illustrious career, he has contributed his voice against oppression and anti-democratic forces, which particularly exposed him to many harrowing experiences during the June 12, 1993 election saga and other professional hazards as a contributor to The National Discourse. The greater danger now, is captured in the attempt to ignore his past professional record and closet his efforts with ethnic slurs, as captured in Baiting Igbophobia: The Sunny Igboanugo Thesis, written by Prof. Wole Soyinka in 2024, as the issues of Peter Obi and his place in the 2023 presidential election rage. This book is therefore a PROTEST!

CONTENTS

PART ONE

THE DRUMBEATS!

For days in early February of 2024, my phone rang ceaselessly. Each caller wanted to know what it was I had to do with Professor Wole Soyinka the poet, storyteller, playwright, essayist, novelist, human rights crusader and ultimately Nobel Laureate – Africa's first in literature. I was totally blank. These were people who had seen the inscription – *Baiting Igbophobia: The Sunny Igboanugo Thesis* being promoted in some social media spaces. It was written by Wole Soyinka.

I had to set off a search party myself after reading the same inscription. I was wondering what it was all about. It was after days of searching that the nickel dropped! It was a book written under the *INTERVENTION SERIES* of the sage. Then another frantic effort set in. It was a frenzy. What was it that the erudite scholar and erstwhile conscience of the nation saw in a lowly Sunny Igboanugo to be worth his ink? Maybe some prank by some people using his name. Again, the nickel dropped. Yinka Oyegbile a versatile journalist and my colleague at both *The Guardian* and *Daily Independent* came to my rescue. Eureka! He had found it! He saw the book! It was on display at the grand event to mark the 50th-anniversary celebration of *The PUNCH*, one of Nigeria's leading newspapers.

Since my friend did not buy a copy for which I nearly ate him raw until he gave me a worthy explanation and had therefore not read the content I had only the title *Baiting Igbophobia: The Sunny Igboanugo Thesis* to contend with. Though I was quite apprehensive given the title which did not smell roses, I took a solemn consolation in the belief that Kongi has his ways with languages and might at best be playing it as only he could. That was until I finally got the copy from *Rovingheights Bookstore* at 28 Ogunlana Drive in Surulere, Lagos. Reading part of it right inside the bookshop my heart practically sank. Melancholy? Yes! It was not praises after all. It was tongue-lashing. Worst of all Kongi was still at it – Peter Obi-bashing! My heart sank further.

Alas! His diatribe was all about a degenerate untrained, indolent, low-life, lying, ethnic-bigot character called Sunny Igboanugo, who was a danger not only to his community but his entire Igbo ethnic group, one who must be punished by first stripping him of his surname Igboanugo (Igbo have heard) because it depicted a generic term suggesting that he was speaking for them. This much I got later from further reading. Of course, he went on to state that that same Igboanugo was not worthy of even the crumbs of bread falling from Wole Soyinka's table where he dines with his class. Let it be known to the world that whatever the sage says about me I accept. I will not argue with him. But I shall tell my story. Here we go!

Unlike the three blind men asked to describe the elephant, most of those who might be asked to describe the historic June 12 1993 presidential election are not blind. That is the major difference. The former is derived from imaginations through just the sense of touch. The latter is a combination of all the senses. I'm part of that story. To a great significant extent. I shall tell mine the way others have been telling theirs over the years.

It began with being part of a group of journalists that travelled from Enugu to Abakaliki. We spent a whole day moving from Enugu to the most interior parts of what is now known as Ebonyi State, which was part of what remained of the old Enugu State after the excision of the present-day Anambra State by Military President Ibrahim Babagida in 1991. Recall that it was the late Nigerian despot, Sani Abacha who carved Ebonyi out of Enugu in 1996. So Ebonyi was in Enugu at that time.

I recall that by the time we returned to Enugu in the evening of that day, we were hardly recognisable. We were all caked in dust. The only human features spared were the eyes – the pupils to be exact and perhaps our voices. The rest including the eyelids were covered in dust casting us otherwise as some strange beings probably emerging from inside strange holes.

To illustrate. How possible is it that dust would penetrate bottles of water inside sealed cartons? But that was exactly our experience. Quite aware of this part of Nigeria and its history with guinea worm we had carried our own water. So, after a long, stressful outing in the field monitoring the process of the election, we had returned to our vehicle to soothe our parched throat. Alas! What did we see when we tore the cartons containing the precious liquids? Nothing was spared! Each bottle of water was filled to half with a deck of dust sediments! Amazing! I'm yet to know how that was possible. Maybe one of these days I would meet a scientist that would explain the strange phenomenon.

For the most part of the June 12 saga after the election was annulled and all through the events that followed, this particular incident continued to play in my mind. I was of course not alone. I remember walking into the office of my namesake, Mr. Sunny Ngwu who I learnt later retired as Commissioner of Police, then the spokesman of the Enugu State Police Command to meet the same sentiment. Throwing his hands in the air in exasperation, the first sentence he uttered was – *Sunny my brother na so that our suffering take go like that?* He was in pain just like any other person who was on that trip to the interiors of Abakaliki and other communities in that enclave.

But like the coinage *Now Your Suffering Continues* used to depict the National Youth Corps Scheme (NYSC) by our ever-witty Nigerians, I never knew rest or slept with my two eyes closed from that moment. Just like many other Nigerians who were either at the centre of gravity or played one role or the other even at peripheral, I had a lot to worry about.

The Guardian the Flagship of Nigerian media which I represented as their reporter in Enugu with eyes on other parts of what is now known as the South East – my unofficial brief from Rutam House made sure of that. While my editors had my feet on the burning coal, my office at Number 23 Edinburgh Road Ogui New Layout Enugu was a rendezvous for all manner of June 12 apologists. It had to do with the status of the paper as the most independent and authoritative at that time.

Of course, that also meant bringing home the ant-infested faggots Chinua Achebe described in his famous book – *Things Fall Apart.* Not only did I become a person of interest to the hordes of goons working for the junta and the dark-goggled despot that office was clearly put on their radar as well. That much I knew.

How many times was I dragged? How many slaps? How many koboko lashes? How many police harassments, invitations and arrests? Yes! The physical pains are gone but not the memory. In fact, recalling some of them leaves me laughing out to myself like that madman at Ajeromi Market in Ajegunle. I recall for instance that particular occasion I was "invited" to Awka by the police command in Anambra State. The late Phanuel Onyedumekwu a chieftain of the Eastern Mandate Union (EMU) who was a principal subject in the eyes of the police – he granted the interview that led to the invitation – came along carrying a mat.

I recall the strange glances other passengers were throwing at him inside the bus we took to Awka as he clutched his mat stoically gazing into empty space in silence while probably ruminating over his impending sure unpalatable fate. Fortunately, this time there was no incarceration or any form of harassment. In fact, the police authorities denied knowledge of the so-called invitation and we had to return to Enugu this time in a more relaxed even hilarious mood.

In another comical episode operatives of the junta were after Nwobodo Onyekwere my colleague from *The PUNCH*. Their informants must have told them that I was the most valuable link given our professional and personal affinity. After days of fruitless search, I was sitting on my desk when my door flew open and a young man stormed in unannounced. Usually, my office assistant would have received him as with all other visitors before coming to inform me. But this particular intruder had no need for that as it could mean tipping me off.

Dressed in mufti, he blew his cover instantly. It came from an involuntary action from the two of us. Always on the edge out of fear of the unknown, I had roared immediately he stepped in – who are you!? Ostensibly out of usual reflexes, he stood at attention immediately. It was a split-second instinctive action before he realised himself. Perhaps his pitch would have been different apparently to cajole me with the usual story that he had an assignment for my friend and needed to contact him. But having exposed himself there was no other need for pretences. He went straight to interrogating me and demanding that I produced the fugitive or see hell. Of course, I stood my ground that I was not Onyekwere's keeper and that it was his job to find him, putting up some bravery even though I was completely filled with trepidation. Remember it was Abacha that we were talking about. Who did not know what this unwelcome chat could lead to? But I stood my ground. After a long war of the eyeballs, my uninvited visitor left but not without warning me that he would be back for an unpleasant handshake. Relief? Understatement!

How many stories will I tell? Okay outside the physical pains what about the psychological torture? One of them had to do with the love of my life then. I recall particularly this event that was the consequence of the proscription of *The Guardian.* Yes! I do not know how many people were in my category in my office but I was among the staff who the company paid their salaries in full for the entire period of hell on earth the proscription lasted. During this period, I was first struck with the reality of journalism in Nigeria – first – as a journalist, you are as relevant and powerful as not only the medium you represent but for the period that you are in its employ. The day you lose that job your phone would stop ringing, apologies, Reuben Abati.

This I experienced first-hand. Not only that virtually all the friends I made particularly in the top echelon of the leadership of the state and more particularly in the political arena disappeared, I was shut out completely from the circle I once enjoyed which was the envy of many. It was a rude shock to discover that the doors that were thrown open in high offices and homes and the warm embraces and accolades had their origin and relevance from the *Flagship* and not me.

But it became messier. My woman had taken a trip to Lagos while I left for Owerri to join my friend in his Business Centre operation at Weatherall Road. I had to leave Enugu in order to minimise the psychological torture of being deserted by my circle of friends including some of my colleagues who took pleasure in my ordeal. The only occasions I returned was to pick up my salary vouchers to pay into the bank to keep soul and spirit together. Of course, the side hustles many journalists engaged in had, become a dead-end. So, I had little reason to continue enduring the loneliness alone when I had an open sesame in Owerri with my friend.

The shock came months after I returned to my job following the de-proscription of the paper. My woman who was always in touch with me at Owerri using the telephone number of my friend at the business centre returned from her Lagos trip. I had wondered why she took so long to make it back to Enugu after my return. That mystery was solved when she eventually came to my office that eventful evening. Nothing would have warned me if not that she came into my arms for the normal squeezing before heading home.

It took a while for me to notice that her stomach was quite hard and that her breasts were bigger, firmer and stronger. Pushing her farther apart I confronted her with what I thought was obvious – you're pregnant? I could recall her giggling about it in her usual breezy hilarious manner of making light of serious issues – the more reason we were soulmates, given that I was also guilty of that characterisation – while not only admitting to the fact but informing me that the traditional wedding activities had been concluded. Betrayal? But I survived. It however meant that I had to add an extra six years before finding a good replacement from the time I was ready to marry now at age 40.

Now does Prof. Wole Soyinka and others revelling in the seductive feeling of June 12 struggle know about this? Certainly no! But this singular event underscores the fact about the multiplicity of such seemingly innocuous narratives by thousands, if not millions of Nigerians who in their own little spaces endure their own scars from that struggle?

Or how would he know about the pressure I faced internally outside the Sani Abacha goons? Recall that Enugu was controlled by the National Republican Convention (NRC) just like Abia and Imo with Anambra being the only state controlled by the Social Democratic Party (SDP) meaning that I was virtually operating in somewhat enemy territory with many lacerating undertakings?

Indeed, the fact that I was not only a June 12 advocate, body and soul, but an acolyte of the late Moshood Kashimawo Olawale (MKO) Abiola made many people unhappy. As I indicated earlier it was not really about me as a person, rather it was the medium I represented – *The Guardian*. So, where the persuasions, supplications and remonstration failed, they were replaced, to a large degree by confrontation, cajoling and outright threats from my brothers who wanted me to bend.

Did the sage know the names I was called and the tag attached to my lapel in some quarters by my brothers and fathers? I was labelled a traitor and saboteur. Some of them reminded me of how the Yoruba where the man I was sticking out my neck for hailed from, betrayed Ndigbo and how this would be an ample opportunity for a payback. Many talked about how the late Chief Obafemi Awolowo, the quintessential Yoruba leader not done with starving millions of my brothers and sisters during the civil war proper, upped the ante by virtually impoverishing the same people financially with the £20 saga.

But, much as historically some of these narratives seemed to have fitted in, I knew that much of their purveyors were simply latching on to them to achieve their individual, but selfish ends altogether. It was all politics in the main. Such sentiments, actually cut little ice with many people outside the political circle and other vested interests. This much was underscored by Abiola's performance in Igboland during the election proper. Even with Sylvester Ugo, who as the Governor of the Central Bank of Biafra, played a central role in the government, as running mate to Bashir Tofa the NRC presidential candidate and opponent of Abiola of the SDP, the same Abiola still swept the entire Igboland in terms of votes. In other words, the primordial sentiments these people were trumpeting had no resonation or rhythm with the ordinary people. If anything, it not only indicated the ability of Ndigbo to heal quickly, but their propensity to treat each case on its own merit. It therefore means that Abiola was Abiola and Awo was Awolowo. None should carry the burden of the other. Certainly, the late Yoruba leader had received his own comeuppance from Ndigbo when it mattered. With the abysmal performance he got from the region when he canvassed for votes under the UPN, Ndigbo had settled their scores with him. Abiola was different and they had to deal with him differently. Besides the younger generation were either not aware or did not bother.

Now let me even narrate my first and chance meeting with MKO. Before the election proper, I had followed him everywhere he went in Igboland as part of his media team covering every meeting private and public, except where such engagements were held behind closed doors. The places he visited and dignitaries he met were legion. I was there when the late Owelle of Onitsha, Dr. Nnamdi Azikiwe broke into some uniquely dainty dance-steps on sighting Kola Animasaun as they sang *ko ile s'ori apata ko ile-ko-ile s'ori apata – ile iyari a ba iyari lo*. I was there at the palace of the late Igwe Osita Agwuna of Enugwu-Ukwu, *Igwe of Umunri* in Anambra State, where the monarch performed some traditional rites on his visitor. I was also there with MKO at the palace of the late Igwe Edward Nnaji the *Odezuruigbo* of Nike. I recall these two prominent monarchs specifically because of the high-octane cultural contents at their palaces.

But I met Abiola in person when he offered me a ride in his personal vehicle on one of the occasions. It was after a campaign meeting at the SDP office in Enugu. A very snobbish woman identified as the coordinator of the campaign in the region had thought it wise to seize the Peugeot 505 station wagon designated for journalists. In her laughable and infantile arrogance, she had asked the reporters to join some of the buses being used by some innocuous groups including women. She could not be bothered by the fact that reporters were a key component of the campaign itself.

You could imagine the snotty gaze she gave me when I confronted her and demanded that the vehicles be returned. I swallowed her derisive downsizing scoff, but insisted that the vehicle would not move without my colleagues in it. In the first place, she was not the one that assigned the vehicle. She was only throwing her weight around. It was during our confrontation, with me literally shouting that MKO overheard and approached me himself to ascertain the cause of the problem. After hearing me, he tried to pull me away to ride with him. *Come come, come and ride in my own vehicle* he had appealed. Of course, I declined the offer – it was really not about me only but the profession, about some people in high places, having this idea of belittling journalists –

and insisted on my earlier position – a step many people not only saw as strange but foolish – *you know what it meant to ride with Abiola* some of them continued to murmur.

How were they to know that that singular incident singled me out in the eyes of the later June 12 winner for which I could have been one of the eventual beneficiaries of the *Hope '93* project had wicked people not poured sands into the garri of millions of Nigerians by denying the country the outcome of that historic election? Yes! That would have been the likely outcome given how close I eventually became with the business mogul, which was even enhanced by his familiarity with my reports on him for which he appreciated. Seeing my determination, MKO and others intervened and the vehicle was released to the journalists.

So how would Kongi know that before Peter Obi and the February 25, 2023, presidential election there was June 12? Come to think of it, how come the June 12 phenomenon has suddenly become an exclusive preserve of the Yoruba with only scant mention of people from other ethnic groups. How come the Igbo components of the struggle either at the electoral stage where prominent Ndigbo played significant roles in making that historic event a reality or in the struggle for the actualisation of Abiola's mandate are seldom mentioned these days?

Why did June 12 become winner takes all of Yoruba people and "we and them" all of a sudden? Granted, the Yoruba were in the forefront of the agitations either at the level of the National Democratic Coalition (NADECO) National Liberation Council of Nigeria (NALICON) and other groups that participated in that struggle. It was natural. However, there were elements from other parts of the country whose actions and contributions were also quite remarkable and ought to be equally celebrated. For instance, how much did his compatriots in the struggle show face during the death of Admiral Ndubuisi Kanu, in solidarity for biting the silver bullet with the others? The last I checked the immortalisation by the Lagos State Government was for his being a one-time military governor and not for his NADECO membership.

What about the likes of Frank Kokori, whom I learnt died in penury, completely deserted on his hospital bed in his last days despite his fiery battle with the Abacha junta for which he spent a substantial part of his life in some of the worst gulags of the despot? Chukwuemeka Ezeife – that ardent and unapologetic proponent of June 12 till his death has since joined the others. What role did NADECO play in his burial and from the foregoing in comforting his family?

What about the late Prof. Humphrey Nwosu, the man that made June 12 happen in the first place? Why the labourious attempt to blot him out from the memory books and from hall of fame? In 2018, when the first national celebration of Abiola took place and the rest, were being mentioned as heroes and June 12 was being designated as *Democracy Day* in Nigeria, he was conveniently sidelined. How could there have been that historic event without the Option A4 which he created and saw through? What manner of history is being made over June 12 without Humphrey Nwosu? What is the argument for treating him so poorly? If for nothing, let the world know where he erred and what his sins and perhaps those of others that have been relegated are. Is it a case of being Igbo hence he did not belong and ought not belong?

So, reading Soyinka's book – *Baiting Igbophobia: The Sunny Igboanugo Thesis* has left me more confused than any form of understanding, knowing my pedigree. I have continued to oscillate between curiosity, confusion, bewilderment and perplexity. What is the connection? This is what I have kept asking myself. What does *Baiting Igbophobia* mean? What is the context? Perhaps the only plausible explanation is Soyinka's ways with words and style. Sometimes, adducing meanings to his expressions, is as difficult as finding the proverbial needle in a haystack – the very reason some people clearly avoided his books in preference to easier readings from other authors in WAEC examinations.

At the time we were reading *The Trials of Brother Jero and Jero's Metamorphosis,* preparatory for the same examination, I knew some people who simply could not cope in spite of the best efforts of our literature teachers. I am told his, is an elevated style for special people – those with deep thinking and ability to deal with the abstract. Well, I do not belong to that class and I will not deceive myself.

So, my understanding of the drift from the title of that book, to its content, is that Kongi attempted to bespatter me with the paintbrush of ethnicity. This conclusion I came to by putting two and two together reading through the aspect that concerned me in the 149-page effort. How he came about this, were it so, I'm yet to understand I dare say for the umpteenth time. If Kongi is looking for anyone to cast in the garb of ethnic champion, I'm the least example.

IGBOPHOBIA? IGBOCENTRIC? NO! I'M A LAGOS BOY!

Anyone seeking knowledge about the structure of Ndigbo as a people, should visit the South East during mass returns usually at the Christmas season. This is not just a period where families and individuals reconnect with their kith and kin, but it is also one to showcase what each individual brought back, not only in terms of materials but far more than that – the culture of other people.

The structures and activities at this period are not only shaped by the distinct categorisations such as individual branches of the town unions of each of the communities, but other conceptual characterisations. So, the man from Sokoto, Kano or Maiduguri is likely to proudly wear his northern attributes like a badge of honour. He would like to be addressed as Alhaji Musa than Okechukwu given to him by his parents before travelling to the North. He is likely to appear at the townhall meeting in his Babariga outfit than his native attire. In a cluster with his colleagues, they are likely to descend into pure Hausa language rather than speaking Igbo.

The man from Osogbo or Ibadan is likely to appear in public in *kembe* and proudly speak Yoruba than Igbo. In Ogboji my home-town in Anambra State, you hear all manner of non-Igbo names adopted by many of my compatriot-returnees for no other reason than that they actually fancy those foreign names and have become accustomed to them. For instance, you are unlikely to find help easily if you told anyone that you are looking for John Okafor my brother-in-law married to my immediate younger sister. But mention Jegede and a child would take you to his house. He has simply substituted his original name with the adopted name he fancies. If you needed a canopy or to book drinks for your events, you are referred to Abiola. Don't make mistakes, he is not Yoruba, but a full-fledged Igbo man who has adopted that name, simply because he likes the sound of it.

Such is the structure of the Igbo society. It is even more so conceptually. Thus, the boys from Enugu, more of a civil service enclave, are supposed to be the well-packaged gentlemen with good dress-sense, neat and well-ordered outlook, high comportment and good manners. Conversely their counterparts from Onitsha, Nnewi, Aba and other commercial towns known more for trading and who are supposed to be the money boys are likely to present the attitude of money-talks-and-bullshit-walks.

They are the loud ones and the ones likely to close popular joints and order special delicacies and pay cash. At this time if you had a beautiful girlfriend, you must guard her closely and better still avoid taking her to such joints if you are not sure of her loyalty to you. Otherwise, you might be dealing with stories that touch the heart.

Then, there are the Lagos boys – the broad-based – cosmopolitan boys – the group that represents everything from street-wisdom to being in touch with modernity, from modern fashion to latest hairstyles. Lagos boys are supposed to be the special breed from where others learn how to flow. That is where I belong. So, given this diverse segmentation of formations and characterisation, it is pretty difficult to force the Igbo society into one pigeonhole, either of ideas or classification.

It is even more so for me. I came to Lagos in 1976 at the age of 12. In that 48-year stretch, I got stuck passing through Lagos and having Lagos pass through me. Where do I really start to relive my Lagos experience? Is it in joining other children of my age in setting bird traps at the Olodi swamp in Ajegunle, joining other street children at Oregie Cinema to discuss the latest film in town including the coming attractions? Is it the street fights or other escapades that we engaged in?

Is it trekking from Ajegunle to the National Stadium in Surulere to watch football matches and the pranks that followed it? A little narration about those pranks. We would get to the stadium very early say around 10 am for a match that would start at 4.45 pm, stay in the queue without the intention of buying tickets. Why that early? Strategic! Business! We knew that some people could not suffer the stress of standing in the queue.

At noon or so the lines would start building up. Someone suddenly walks up to you and a bargain is soon concluded. Just five kobo and the space would be his. You moved back to the rear. Getting close to the centre of the queue now stretching longer another person comes this time the stake increases. Time is 1.30 pm. Price – 15kobo. Back to the rear. Then 2.45-3 pm you sell again this time 30kobo. Then 4 pm the boys from Idumota rush in. How much? Money exchanges hands space vacated. Price - 50kobo. By the time the first roar of the crowd is heard outside indicating the emergence of the players, you are probably N1.50 richer. Yet, you either found your way by pleading with the bouncers at the gate or clambered the floodlight pole to get into the stadium. This was Lagos, my Lagos. Did *Baba* Soyinka know this much about me to closet me in that airtight ethnic jacket?

But these are the tiny stories. What about the bigger ones? Did Kongi know for instance that I enjoyed full free education in Lagos, a Yoruba land? Yes! From textbooks, exercise books, pencils, erasers, math-sets, pens, rulers – everything was provided for that little Igbo boy whose name was and is still Igboanugo, just in the same manner as it was for Olarenwaju Ajayi, a Yoruba, Aaron Essien, an Isoko, Odafe Oserada an Urhobo, Inelagwu Onche from Benue. Yes! Nobody got anything different because he was Igbo and nobody got his own a day earlier or after because he was Hausa. Not even the daughter of the principal got hers earlier than another student.

To be sure the name of my school is Awori College Ojo, a walking distance to Alaba International Market and Lagos State Government College, now housing the premises of the Lagos State University (LASU). By the way, that was how I was cocksure that it was impossible for anybody to have attended the college in 1970, because I knew Awori College was established in 1975, a year after Lagos State Government College. I was completely exasperated by the claim, were it truly made by President Bola Tinubu, as they claimed the Chicago saga revealed.

So, in the main, it is impossible for me to take positions on issues in Nigeria because I'm Igbo. Mind my words I'm not saying it is difficult, I mean IMPOSSIBLE. There is too much Lagos blood in me to begin to think or act along that line. How could I, living and experiencing the Lagos of that time, which desperate people are now trying to deface and disgrace? A Lagos of Lateef Jakande, where Lagos was a home for all, a land of push and opportunities where both tricksters like Prof. Kpambo operating at Mile 2 bus stop, side by side with the hustlers at the Apapa and Tincan Wharfs, the young managers at the thriving companies in the construction, trading and manufacturing, as well as the top middle-level and low-grade workers, daily in search of one thing – opportunities.

No Sir! Egbon Kongi! I'm a Lagos boy. That means in this context, I'm neither Igbo, Hausa or Yoruba. Just Lagos boy. Did I not attend the party when one of my kinsmen won one of the flats at FESTAC town? Okay, that was a federal project. But I also knew about those who won the Jakande houses, some of them my Igbo brothers, just like other non-Yoruba indigenes. You know what? Many of them did not even know anyone or go anywhere. They just applied by following the process only to find their names in the *Evening Times* that they had won.

Yes! They won permanent homes in Lagos – the heart of Yoruba land without greasing palms and without knowing anyone. For all you know, they could have been members of the Nigerian Peoples Party (NPP) the Igbo-dominated platform due to the influence of Nnamdi Azikiwe the late Owelle of Onitsha. Yet, it did not prevent anything or count against them under the government of the Unity Party of Nigeria (UPN) led by Chief Obafemi Awolowo a Yoruba man. Could Awo not have decreed and Jakande the *Baba Kekere* – Awo's replica obeying, ensured that all beneficiaries of that largesse must be Yoruba or at the least members of the UPN. Why did they have to throw open the contest for everyone? That is the society I know because it was what I grew up in.

There are countless such big stories about Lagos, in virtually all aspects of that era, which I still cling to so stubbornly today, believing that the attempt to destroy the essence of what the Jakandes of yesterday's Lagos left behind would soon vanish for the environment of plural, vigorous, thriving society to return. That Lagos is what makes me happy. It represents the meaning of a good liveable society to me. I could not trade it for anything.

How could I? Would I deny or erase the memories I shared with my friends whose ethnicity or parentage meant virtually nothing as we sat together to eat our afternoon meals, the sweetest that I ever tasted? Yes! Outside going to school totally free, Jakande or should I say Awo, fed me also. For five years of my life in the most crucial days of my formative years that shaped my total being today. It was either a choice between rice, beans, and or asaro (special yam porridge).

Why should I leave that life of freedom for the asphyxiating cage-life of ethnicity? Yes! I'm Igbo, the type of Igbo the late Ikemba Nnewi used to call *Igbogborigbo*. I love being Igbo. I love the food, the life, the society, the community. I love particularly Ogboji my home town. I love the environment, the bushes, the streams, the springs and the soil – the virginity. But I love something more – the life of freedom I found in Lagos and its diversity. That life was there in the street. You didn't need to bend down to see it. It stared you in the face.

It was there in that local bakery owner, who routinely fed us with hot freshly-baked bread whenever we trekked past her bake-house and paused to savour the sweet aroma wafting through that makeshift structure. She never cared to ask us where we came from or who our parents were. All she saw were children with their school bags hung on their shoulders passing by, doing their own things in their own world. They could probably be her own children.

Make no mistake about it, Lagos was also a risky place – strewn with a lot of dangers. There were also bad people everywhere – robbers who could kill without any cause, fraudsters who duped the wealthy and brought them down, landlords who punished their tenants and tenants who took their landlords to court and refused to pay rents or bolted away after owing for months or years. The evil you could find in Lagos could dry up the Atlantic or transform the Sahara Desert to an ocean.

Yet, beneath that and beyond the sad stories, were the legions of delightful showcasing of humanity, in which the man sitting next to a child would pay his transport fare just for seeing him as his or the utterly cantankerous bus conductor would get in harm's way just to prevent a group of touts from harassing a young woman. It is this seeming contradiction, if not complexity that gave Lagos that alluring breath of life and made it for me. The new Lagos the bad guys have struggled to build over the years, particularly in these years of the APC in power, is an anathema as much as bad for the health.

But it is not even just about Lagos. In those days of my formative years, I also made some considerable inroads into some Yoruba towns. This came about with the sudden discovery of Osogbo as a new destination of economic hub for my kits in my village. My immediate elder brother was one of those who established his local clothing business in that town, then still under Oyo State. Osogbo made such an economic impact on my people that it became a major centre of attraction. You began to hear the mantra – *o ndi Osogbo* – they are Osogbo people just as you heard about Lagos, Enugu, Onitsha et al.

With my brother gaining freedom from his master who took him to Osogbo and establishing his own business, it became a routine for me to camp there with him to spend my holidays. And what did I do then? First, it was completely out of the question for a healthy young man to stay at home while others battled with the elements outside to feed the stomach. So, I joined in the business naturally. It meant that each morning a thick load of trouser materials was fitted on my head for the market.

Of course, the market was not just one location but the streets. It was not even in Osogbo town but far-flung communities within and beyond – as far-flung as Ikirun, Ikire, Ede, Iwo, Ilesa. I trudged the streets of these towns with loads on my neck and what I found was no markedly different from the treatment of strangers in Awka, Ekwulobia, Afikpo, Obingwa, Okigwe or any other Igbo community, where you were welcomed with the hospitality of the locals. If not, the former was far more welcoming. So where would I have to pick up the trait of ethnicity uncle WS tried to cloak me in? What I have been labouring to say from the foregoing is that if Kongi is looking for an ethnic culprit I represent the wrongest example!

Presently, I'm at the stage where Kongi was some 20-50 years ago, where he tried to stop the moving train with his bare hands and looked the bulls, tigers, lions and bears in the corridors of power in Nigeria eyeball to eyeball and confronting them with such raw courage only very few in the world could boast about. That is where I am today. Just as he stood tall at that time and spoke truth to power, I wish to also enjoy the feeling.

True, mine might not be as loud, it might even be inaudible and ineffective compared to that of the WS of *The Man Died* fame, but tiny as it is, I still own it and I must express it in my little space, one in which I dare not only own completely but savour the alluring feeling. In fact, this was exactly my sermon to those who confronted me in those days of the June 12 saga. While wondering where I derived the power and courage to dare, I had always told them freedom to tell the truth, remained the greatest asset mankind could possess. Even so, my usual counsel had always been don't try to be like me. Just condemn the impunity even in your personal closet. In your small corner of your room just say what these people did is not good. That way, you would have exculpated yourself from the nagging consequences of guilt, borne by the enablers of that construct even if you were not directly involved.

Yes! I may lack the courage of Kongi in pulling a gun to cause the announcement of an election in Western Nigeria or against all counsel, take a trip to enemy territory and confer with a supposed rebel leader, waging war against Nigeria and ending up in jail as a result, but I'll make up for that in that my little corner with my tiny voice. I shall speak! And by God, I shall speak the truth as I know it!

Perhaps when I climb the seventh floor of my life or the ninth floor where Kongi is at the moment, things might change. That is if the proverbial snake which I suspect has bitten my revered sage eventually whips me with its tail. For the only explanation that anyone like me could glean from or adduce for the present-day Kongi, is that there might be something in the older generation that blunts the sharp edges of eagerness. There is really something on that floor capable of making the tiger shed its tigritude, an element that has led to the obvious transformation WS seems to have undergone.

Indeed, on one of the numerous occasions I had a sit-down with the late Ikemba at his number 4 Isi-Uzor Crescent Independent Layout Enugu, I posed a question to him as we were reviewing his Biafran efforts. I asked him if he was going to act in exactly the same manner he did in the build-up and through the prosecution of the war with Nigeria. Ojukwu took a long look at me with his eyeballs bulging as usual and quipped "how would you expect me as an old man in my 70s to act in the same manner as I did in my 30s?"

That witty response remained quite apparent in the perspective as I followed most of his undertakings in the remaining parts of his life, including the crisis that engulfed the All Progressives Grand Alliance (APGA), the party he was called to lead after it was founded by Chekwas Okorie in 2002 and through which he contested twice for the President of Nigeria – 2003 and 2007.

Let me stress this. It is a popular tale in my hood, used to adumbrate how age could affect views and conducts. It is the story of a certain notorious thief, who had stolen a cock but was discovered by a group of children who followed him with the intention of retrieving it from him. In the commotion that ensued a passer-by, an old man was soon invited to intervene in the situation. The said thief trying to seize the chance to not only avoid the embarrassment but possible lynching, implored the passer-by to check into his goatskin bag "with the eyes of an old man" to see if there was any fowl in it.

Of course, understanding the danger the thief was in and apparently electing to help him save his skin, the old man looked into the bag and told the children to disperse because what they thought was a fowl was something else. Of course, he succeeded in dispersing the children but he also chided the thief before forcing him to release the fowl. Thus, it was a win-win situation. If only Kongi had succeeded in creating the same win-win by making those who stole the Nigerian fowl let go, his transformation from the fire-eating crusader to the white-haired sage adept at looking into a bag with the eyes of an old man could have been more understandable.

The quarrel is that he is not only insisting that there is no stolen fowl in the bag but has also failed to cause the release of its content. Now the fowl is on its way to facing the inevitable sad end. Its squeaking from the sealed bag continues as a sad reminder that soon it will be slaughtered, decapitated, cooked and eaten. Would Kongi exculpate himself from this sad fate? I dare ask. Would he escape from the record of tomorrow's history as an enabler to this sad destiny? How sad a history it would be for the very world celebrated Nigerian hero.

BIAFRA? WHAT ABOUT IT?

Nothing, since the event more than 50 years ago, has provided a tool to ensnare the feet of Ndigbo in Nigeria than Biafra. Naysayers have used it as a convenient excuse to instigate, promote and nurture all manner of negative agendas against them. To say the least, Ndigbo, have found themselves in the same foggy and smelly condition as Jonah in the belly of the wale for decades since this unfortunate incident in Nigeria's history. But nothing compares to their current experience under the APC government, which came into power in 2015. Muhammadu Buhari, the first President on the platform of the party, actually made it a sport to deal with Ndigbo in the biblical description of flogging the people with snakes and scorpions. Much as the people, for whom the sentiment was mutual against Buhari, felt that the coming of President Bola Tinubu, would provide some sort of elixir, if not change their parlous condition totally, given his initial chummy disposition with the people of the South East, as Governor of Lagos State, nothing has happened in that regard. If anything, Tinubu, though not as frontal as Buhari, has continued on that anti-Igbo trajectory and in some cases, upped the ante. For one, he has ensured that Ndigbo are well kept away from the dinner table. He has practically erected a glass ceiling to ensure that Ndigbo watched, while the rest of Nigerians are having their sumptuous banquets.

It is so painful that Soyinka, a major player in that sad episode in Nigerian history, seems to have caught the anti-Igbo bug. He has not only kept silent in the build-up to, and pendency of this tyranny, but in certain ways, by words and deeds, promoted it, to the extent that many now believe that *The Man Has Died in Him.*

If it would help, let me present one of the episodes, to under-score how Ndigbo have become a specimen for demonstration of this prejudice, if not apartheid in their own country.

Read:

People agitate everywhere even in my house. The first thing you do with an agitator is to sit down and listen to the person who is agitating. Unless you sit down you cannot say yes or no. I'm a Ni-gerian. I'm contesting election in Nigeria. I'm not contesting from any other place. I'm a Nigerian I believe in Nigeria. I believe in the unity of Nigeria and I believe that I'm going to bring all agitators back to Nigeria and make it work for them because the reason they're agitating is injustice. When you provide justice for them – justice equity and create a level-playing field where people are happy there won't be agitations.

Don't forget there were agitations yesterday in America (Ameri-can Civil War). Don't think America was like this before. There was agitation before in Brazil. I can show you countries where there were so many agitations. But when level-playing fields were created with talents marching opportunities all these things would go.

These were the words of Peter Obi the presidential candidate of the Labour Party (LP) in the February 2023 presidential elec-tion. It was his response to the question posed to him about the agitation for the creation of the state of Biafra by some people in the South East principally through the Indigenous People of Biafra (IPOB). It was during his appearance at *The Candidate* an audience-participation television interview, hosted by Kadaria Ahmed with presidential candidates for the election.

One Rahman Hadeza from Bayero University Kano (BUK) had asked him if he believed in the Biafran agitation and wanted him a yes or no answer. The above words were his response. Before then one Abubakar Sadiq who was a member of the audience in the studio at the event said to have been supported by the Mark Arthur Foundation had asked a similar question that seemed to point a direct link between him and the Eastern Security Network (ESN) an outfit believed to be the enforcement arm of IPOB.

Question:

My question is very direct and I'll like Mr. Peter Obi to answer it directly. A day after Anambra State Governor Charles Soludo critisised the mode and style of your government his home town was attacked by the ESN. How does this portray your claim to freedom of expression without fear of people being maimed or killed? If you eventually emerge as president people will criticise, are we going to be safe?

Response:

If you follow our seven-point agenda the first one is to secure and unite Nigeria. It is our commitment to secure the lives and property of Nigerians and to ensure a united and one Nigeria.

How? (From Kadiria)

Response:

By ensuring that there is equity justice and doing things following the rule of law. If you check my utterances everywhere or Datti

Baba-Ahmed's own you'll not see where we made statements like – don't vote these people because they're from here or statements like somebody said – I'll send Peter back to where he's coming from. We're people who are all over the place.

I come from the South East I'm in Lagos I'm in the South East I'm in Abuja and travelled everywhere and I've maintained that nobody should vote for me because it is my turn. And I've maintained it. I have lived it. As governor, the closest person to me was my ADC. My ADC is from Kano. I always say he is the best policeman I've ever met. We remain close till today.

Kadiria:

Somebody in the audience asked a specific question on the attack on Governor Soludo and I want to add to that by asking you specifically what you make about the agitation from the South East specifically your position on IPOB and ESN.

Response:

Everyone knows my position on those issues. I've said I'll dialogue and discuss with all agitators. Everywhere in the country is full of agitation. These are the cumulative effect (effects) of leadership failure over the years. There is nothing wrong with agitation. We'll dialogue and discuss with everybody.

Kadiria:

What about the attacks and the killings?

Response:

What he said has no correlation. To be fair I've taken a position on Soludo and said he's my governor and my senior brother and we're very close. What he said is his opinion. You cannot be at-

tacking people for speaking their opinions. Otherwise, we'll be attacking everybody on the road every day. Do you know how many people that tell me that you don't know what you're doing? I would have attacked you self. I've never knowingly as Peter used bad language on anybody.

Kadiria:

So can you condemn ESN for the attacks and the killings in the South East?

Response:

No I cannot condemn because I'm not sure about who is doing what. You cannot just be condemning people until somebody says these are the evidence. People say all sorts of things. You can only condemn people when there is a process where somebody proves that this person has done this.

Kadiria:

So, you do not believe the security services when INEC offices are attacked when people have been killed – the late Dora Akunyili lost her husband and they say it is ESN – you don't believe it?

Response:

Let me tell you I singlehandedly left Lagos without any single security took first flight to Owerri drove to Ogidi Police Station to retrieve the body of Chike Akunyili. Nobody did. I singlehandedly did. Dora and I everybody knows – I was the last person to visit Dora Akunyili in her hospital in India before she died. I'm very close to Dora and the family and everybody knows. But I can't tell you what happened to Chike Aknunyili and nobody can say it is this person or that person.

Chike Akunyili was just trying to drive back to Enugu and ran into people who were robbing and doing all sorts of things in circumstances nobody can explain. Even when he was trying to say stop this stop that of course he was shot. But you see whenever things like that happens (happen) people speculate all sorts of things. Nigeria is a place where people speculate on everything.

Kadiria:

Because there is research that shows a direct correlation between the formation of ESN some of the pronouncements of Nnamdi Kanu about take their guns and shoot their guns and people are saying if the witch cries at night and the baby dies in the morning, we know who killed the baby.

Response:

I have about 10 messages here saying I should not come to your programme because you are totally against me. But I'm here. I told them and said I like visiting people who are totally against me. If I take all those views I won't be here. I'll like to see that witch before I call it witch.

When asked to make his closing pitch Obi told his audience:

Two of us have appealed to Nigerians next election should not be based on tribe. No tribe buys bread cheaper or have better roads or anything. It should not be based on religion because no religion is buying bread cheaper or has been able to employ everybody. It should not be based on it is my turn. It is the turn of every Nigerian to take back their country. We have made a promise we will secure and unite this country.

We have promised. We will ensure that we will move Nigeria from consumption to production start pulling people out of poverty. We will ensure we will work with the rule of law deal with the issue of corruption where we will bring it to a minimal level. We will govern from the front. We will be in charge and we will make Nigeria work where we have Nigeria but we don't have Nigerians we will create Nigerians who will be proud of their country because we will be in charge. The buck will stop at our desk. We will work as brothers. No team will in this equation can beat our team.

Those words were supposed to seal it and present Obi for what he had laboured to convince Nigerians as to who he truly is, especially when no contrary evidence came from anybody outside mere words of propaganda. Like the canary, he sang it like a song: *Don't vote for me because I'm Igbo but because I'm a Nigerian.* Yet they never let go. Please note that no other candidate was taken up on the issue of ethnic issues or agitations.

A month after Kadira's interview in November 2022, specifically on Monday, October 17 2022, at a conference organised by the Arewa joint committee for presidential candidates, it was Obi's task to speak on the same issue this time, in response to the allegation made against him by Nasir el-Rufai, former Governor of Kaduna State, who called him a tribalist. To prove it, the former Minister of the Federal Capital Territory (FCT), had recounted how Obi had ordered his arrest and detention inside his hotel while on a mission for the APC then one of Nigeria's opposition parties during the 2013 governorship election in Anambra State.

In flatly debunking the allegation Obi had this to say:

Number one, in my eight years of being governor only in the first three months did I have a commissioner that is not from the north — commissioner of police – and that's because I met the person.

At the time the governor said this it was during election. The police commissioner that was there then was from Adamawa — CP Gwari from Adamawa. The AIG that supervised that election was CP Nasarawa from the north. The DIG that came for that election was from Kano.

Tell me my power that I was in APGA—government was PDP and APC. Tell me how an APGA person will issue order for somebody to be detained. Even me was detained in my local government. However, the only offence I committed is that when they asked me I said 'That's how they treat everybody; that I wouldn't be in Kaduna on the day of election'. That was the only thing.

There is no way. I cannot do that. As governor of Anambra State, I had the best ADC in Nigeria—the best policeman. My ADC Mohammed is from Kano. He's the best policeman that I have ever met. Who will I give the order? How will I tell who lives in my house every day; I'm close to his family; I get up and say 'Mohammed I want to deal with your people'.

In fact, a month before September 21, 2022, to be precise, Shehu Mahdi, a medical doctor and self-acclaimed activist, but more of a northern exponent, who moved into the campaigns of Atiku Abubakar, former Nigerian Vice President and the Peoples Democratic Party (PDP) candidate, had presented a more frontal attack in this direction.

It did not matter to the vocal commentator on national affairs that the selfsame Obi was the running mate of the same Atiku in the 2019 presidential effort. Would the implication of his pushing Obi as a tribal bigot and an advocate of Biafra an interesting contradiction and ironic commentary on not only Atiku's image as a nationalist but one capable of headhunting like minds in projecting and promoting national unity? Could the Waziri Adamawa have chosen a Biafran irredentist as his deputy?

But, in politics, everything is fair-game, they say. So, Mahdi, at a meeting, had in a video that went viral directed a specific message to Christians in the region warning them about the dangers of voting Obi into power, the reason once again being that it would be akin to handing over power to—wait for it—a Biafran.

Here are his exact words:

This is a message to my Northern Christian brothers and sisters. It is specifically for you. Why? Because if you go to the South South, to the South East, to the South West, a Christian from the Northern part of Nigeria is a Northerner. Simple! If there is a breakdown of law and order in Enugu, they kill everybody whether a Christian or Muslim coming from the North. This is a record that is on the ground. Nobody can deny this.

Christians of Northern extraction think wisely, act wisely, behave wisely. You have no business voting a Southern candidate based on Christianity. At the end of the day, his agenda is not you. His agenda is his own tribe. If you pick Obi, his agenda is not Christianity – he could be a fantastic Catholic – but beyond the truth is that he is a diehard Biafran. If you put Obi, you are voting for Biafra. There is no mincing of the words. If you vote for Biafra, you are voting for the destruction of the North. Tell me a Christian from Taraba, Nasarawa, Kogi, Kwara, Kaduna, Kebbi, Sokoto, Bauchi, Gwombe, tell me the benefit you will derive by voting Obi. Just tell me one single benefit. And the answer is there is none.

If you want to know if the answer is true, go to Enugu, go to Aba, go to Nnewi, go to Akwa Ibom, go to every part of the South as a Christian and ask for a land to build a church. I think Christianity is supposed to be universal. Go and ask for land to build a church there as a Northern Christian. You will never have one. You will never have one. But all over the North, here are churches owned by who—from the people from the South.

The land is owned by them, the church is owned by them, you go to these churches for service, you give the tithes to them. They are feeding fat, growing fat on you as Christian brothers belonging to the body of Christ. But you don't know that they belong to different Christianity. Go over there and ask for a land to build a church, not even a mosque.

Indigenous Muslims from the South now are building mosques with their hard(-earned) money with a lot of intimidation from the governments—a lot. We give them a lot of accommodation, but they are not thinking Nigeria. Obi is not thinking Nigeria, quote me anywhere, any day, anytime.

From the foregoing, it is not difficult to establish that part of the grand plan by his opponents, some certain established tendencies, and entrenched interests across the country to push back the groundswell of momentum, break the electrifying current within and outside the shores of the land, and/or quench the burning fire, was to cast Obi in the ethnic garb not just as an Igbo irredentist but supposedly the worst form of it—Biafra.

No doubt these interests must have been scared stiff with the Obi momentum at that time and sought for a means of dousing it. What more could be more potent than Biafra?

Godwin Obaseki Governor of Edo State, was in fact one of the first voices to echo out the Obi phenomenon and the earthquake it would bring to the Nigerian politics.

Hear him:

The future of our politics in this country is changing. I don't know how you are, whether you are closely watching what is going on with the level of disenchantment with the existing parties. I'm sure in all our homes, we have so many people now who call themselves Obidients. I don't know whether you have them in your house. Just ask them all those children which party you are for, and they will say Obidient. Do you understand? They don't want us. They're not talking about APC or PDP. They're looking for alternatives. And they're much, much more. You see all of them queuing for PVCs now. They're not looking in the direction of APC or PDP. They're looking for alternatives. If we don't make our party attractive, I don't know what will happen to us in this country.

What else could be more potent to trigger off fear within the established interests? That the likes of El-Rufai and Mahdi would get to work is therefore understandable. Of course, there were many more like these two who represented the frontline warriors and champions of the ethnic campaigns from the national down to the family levels. There were also a host of other less vocal, but equally valuable agents of the campaign, who wanted to stop the moving train using every aspect of human interaction to spread the propaganda. But how far did it go?

The success or futility of the ugly, divisive propaganda was underscored by the somewhat verbal war that ensued between El-Rufai and the Obidients as to who owned the Kaduna streets. It began with the governor, in his usual haughty manner, scoffing, sniggering, and generally dismissing the Obidients in one of his outings. In the days of the million-man matches where the group seized the streets across the country not only to mobilise but also to demonstrate their strength and the fact that they meant business, El-Rufai's obvious move to pour cold water on their efforts, had dared the group to come to Kaduna. In that now infamous tweet of Monday, August 15, 2022, he mockingly declared that the LP movement would not garner up to 200 followers, mostly imports from the South East, riding on night buses to the state due to their inability to open their shops on Mondays.

Pun intended, he wrote:

In Kaduna? Not Kaduna Twitter? I hope you get Two Hundred persons on the streets, including those 'imports' that can't open their shops on Mondays and came on an overnight bus last night!! I jus' dey laff wallahi tallahi!! – @KadunaResident.

He was that confident. He must have been cocksure that with the level of work, he had done to bend the minds of the people to hate Obi and his campaign, the deed was done, and the Kaduna effort would fall flat on its face.

Eventually, when the Kaduna edition of the street mobilisation held on October 1, 2022, after several weeks of delays, intrigues, and threats, it was far from the picture of less than 200 people El-Rufai painted. Rather, the outcome was a direct opposite, as Kaduna people came out in droves as if to pass a verdict against their governor.

The reason for the stunning success was not far-fetched. Kaduna, like other Nigerians, also caught the bug. Those who did not hear, were made to hear by the heavy mobilisation that took place. Jemima Ebrega, the team lead, Youth in Diaspora Coalition (YIDC), one of the several groups mobilising for the event, captured the prevailing sentiments when she argued that Obi was the only presidential candidate capable of salvaging Nigeria from the parlous situation it found itself in.

Just like many other volunteers across the country who employed their personal resources in the mobilisation effort, Ebrega was seen in viral videos, distributing aprons she made with her money free to traders in Kaduna markets, to enable them to identify the LP logo during the election.

That Kaduna became one of the states in the North that produced a lawmaker for the LP despite the odds, was indeed, further proof of the futility of El-Rufai's attempt at the Biafran angle narrative. Of course, that outcome in itself was not a tea party.

It came with sorrow, tears and blood. For instance, on Tuesday, November 29, 2022, news broke that Victoria Chintex was dead. Chintex was the woman leader of the LP in the state. She was one of the backbones for the massive mobilisation activities of the party and largely responsible for the inroads it was making then. She was reportedly shot dead in her home in Kaura, a suburb of the Kaduna metropolis.

Edward Buju, publicity secretary of the LP in Southern Kaduna Senatorial Zone, who broke the story a day after the incident, wrote in a statement:

The Southern Kaduna (Zone 3) Labour Party commiserate with the party chairman and his exco's in Kaura Local Government Area over the untimely demised [demise] of our mother and sister Mrs. Victoria Chintex, woman leader Kaura Local Government, who [was] killed yesterday (Monday) by some unknown gunmen [gunmen] n her resident in Kaura.

Mrs. Chintex was an industrious, hardworking, and dedicated party leader. We are saddened by the unfortunate incident coming at a time when people like her are needed to champion the course [cause] for a new nation through the LP. We call on members of the LP at all levels in the state to pray for the repose of her soul.

"More so as we await the burial plans by the family, the Zone 3 LP will make support to her family. On behalf of our Presidential candidate Peter Obi, our gubernatorial candidate in Kaduna State Jonathan Asake, the party senatorial candidate for Southern Kaduna Senatorial zone Mike Auta, we call on the people of Kaura LGA to be law-abiding as vengeance is of the Lord..."

That this gruesome murder came at a time the LP and its supporters were still relishing the euphoria from the success of the Kaduna rally, which had the imprimatur of the deceased led to the obvious finger-pointing. It was a case of the witch crying in the night and the baby dying in the morning. Naturally, it was greeted with profound outrage. Obi, in a tweet, while bewailing the development, said it was the more reason he would pursue his ambition with greater vigour, so as to nip the problem of insecurity in the bud.

He wrote:

I am shocked by the mindless killing of Mrs. Victoria Chintex, the Labour Party's women leader in Kaura, Kaduna State by yet to be identified gunmen. Her death is a huge loss to her immediate and extended family and to our Labour Party. She lives on in our hearts. May the soul of the late Mrs. Victoria Chintex rest in perfect peace. My sincere condolences to her family. Her killing and the loss of many innocent lives across the nation to gunmen and terrorists are the reasons why I must prioritise the war against insecurity as my first task in office. We must not allow the waste of human lives in Nigeria under any guise.

Even the killing of no fewer than 28 persons in Malagum and Sokwong communities in Kaura Local Government Area of the state a week after, was seen in the light of the circumstances of Chintex's assassination, as both the Christian Association of Nigeria (CAN) and the LP pointed accusing fingers in the same direction.

Rev. John Joseph Hayab, CAN chairman in the state who conveyed the feelings of his people in a statement, alluded that it was politically motivated. Expressing deep regret over the incident, he lashed out at the state government.

He said:

Those who committed this evil must be fished out, arrested, and brought to face justice. These renewed killings may be a strategy to scare the people from exercising their rights and to further increase fear and impoverish them. Accordingly, CAN condemns this barbaric act in the strongest terms but appeal for calm, calling on the government and security to rise to the duty of protecting lives and property.

Umar Farouk Ibrahim Mai Rakumi, LP national secretary, was more frontal.

In his own words:

Our great party has noticed with dismay in recent times the spate of killings of our party supporters in Kaduna State. Particularly in southern Kaduna, which is one of our strongholds and the constituency of our gubernatorial candidate, Hon Jonathan Asake, is becoming a source of concern. Just last week, our great party lost eight members in Kaura local government and Zangon Kataf local government areas respectively. This series of killings within a short time is highly condemnable and insensitive, especially in this festive period.

Our great party strongly condemns these killings, and we cannot continue folding our arms seeing our members killed on a daily basis. As such, we call on the Kaduna State government to do all it takes to bring the perpetrators of this heinous act to book.

We in the Labour Party want the Kaduna State government to be proactive in protecting the lives and property of the citizens. We also call on the Kaduna State government to as a matter of urgency put all the mechanisms in motion, apprehend, and prosecute whoever has [a hand] in this criminality.

The killing of the amiable woman leader of Labour Party in Kaduna State, Mrs. Victoria Chintex, is still fresh in our minds, and we will follow up with her gruesome murder till the Kaduna State government apprehends the culprits. Her husband who was attacked in the process is still receiving treatment as we wish him a speedy recovery.

Instructively, nowhere was either Biafra or Obi mentioned in these grisly incidents. Samuel Aruwan, commissioner for internal security and home affairs, conveying El-Rufai's deep sorrow on the development, quoted him as describing the carnage, which he attributed to the handiwork of bandits operating in the area, as inhuman considering the efforts of government, security forces, the traditional institution, and other critical stakeholders within the last week. So why not Biafra? What else does anyone need to establish that neither Biafra nor Obi is the issue and that for every finger being pointed in that direction, four others pointed in the direction of the real culprits?

Yet this is the same circle Kongi has fallen into, wittingly or unwittingly, and at this stage of his life.

This is the tragedy! What makes WS believe that at the mention of Biafra, every Igbo man would flinch? Certainly not Sunny Igboanugo.

Yes, Biafra! What about it? Every Igbo is a Biafran. In fact, any Igbo man that denies not being one should have his bloodline checked. But this Biafra is not the one that the likes of Mahdi, El-Rufai, and now Soyinka are projecting. It is not the Biafra of scaremongering. Ojukwu described it quite aptly—Biafra of the mind and not of territory. This is the Biafra that makes every Igbo man a global citizen, that makes him resilient enough to dare the seven seas and seven forests to succeed. It is the Biafra of wishing no one ill and doing no one harm.

It is that Biafra that makes a 17-year-old boy on a trip to Osogbo during school break to, rather than enjoying the luxury of easy life and sleep, hit the streets of Ikirun, Ikire, Ogbomoso, and Ede with loaded trousers materials on his head without fears of any sort of harm. It is the Biafra that makes the Gala-seller to mimic Usen Bolt, as he races towards moving vehicles in the streets of Ikeja or Benin just to rake up capital to hire a little stall in a corner of a street, from where he transforms himself into a business mogul years later, by applying an early life of discipline and resilience. It is what compels him to decide to eat his meal without meat at that *mama put* joint while his mates he started life with, garnish their morning peppered rice with *orisirisi*.

It is the Biafra of little beginnings – that impels the young lad whose master had just settled after six years of apprenticeship to gather his few belongings in a sack and head to that far-flung space of uncharted quarters, to set up and by providing the people of his new habitation with what they need, soon becomes a prominent member of that community because he diligently paid his dues. Yes! It is that Biafra that makes the Igbo man compete with natives outside his land on who would build the most beautiful houses, because he has wittingly adopted his hosts as his—wearing their clothes, eating their foods, taking their titles, marrying their daughters or having his own daughters marry them.

Yes! The Biafra of live and let live, of the life of the eagle and the kite finding space to perch on the same tree and the heavens, causing the wing of the one trying to prevent the other from perching to wither; of the life of the fish and the life of the river— where the fish should not die and the river should not dry—of justice, equity, and fair play. This is the Biafra I'm guilty of.

The other Biafra Kongi is trying to clothe me with is not mine. It belongs to outsiders like Muhammadu Buhari who as patrons created, packaged, and decorated that strange Biafra for sale to the unwary.

IPOB, THEIR IPOB; BIAFRA, THEIR BIAFRA

Yes! In one of his accounts on *Baiting Igbophobia: The Sunny Igboanugo Thesis*, Kongi spoke about how he called Buhari out for proscribing IPOB without meting out the same treatment to Fulani herdsmen reputed then to be the harbinger of death in many parts of the country. Of course, the genesis of what has become the recent hoopla about Biafra using IPOB as the agent, has its origin from what the Kongi is pointing – the mindset of different strokes for different folks.

Premium Times reported how in 2016 more than 1,269 people were killed in just Benue State alone in attacks linked to the deadly Fulani group. Add this to the 40 reportedly killed in Dori and Mesuma villages in Gashaka Local Government Area of Taraba or the 40 others massacred in Nimbo, Uzor Uwani Local Government Area of Enugu State. That is when you begin to get the argument.

But it gets more interesting as the picture of the true IPOB and the contrived IPOB begins to appear, when mirrored further. Before its proscription on September 20, 2017, was it ever reported anywhere that IPOB members shot a single person or engaged in kidnapping or any other forms of criminal activities? The highest crime they committed was bearing placards for which scores of youths in the streets of Onitsha stopped bullets with their bare chests.

To underscore how important the matter was to him, Buhari had to come through an executive order to proscribe IPOB. It was even so urgent that a session had to be held inside the chambers of the Federal High Court Abuja, through an ex parte motion, with the accused persons absent, to place a permanent seal on it.

The late Abdul Kafarati of the Federal High Court Abuja, who presided over the matter, granted all the reliefs sought as canvassed by Abubakar Malami (SAN), Attorney General and Minister of Justice (AGF-MoJ), and Dayo Apata, Solicitor General of the Federation (SGF) and Permanent Secretary of the Federal Ministry of Justice alongside other lawyers from the ministry.

For emphasis, hear what he decreed:

That an order declaring that the activities of the respondent (Indigenous People of Biafra) in any part of Nigeria, especially in the South-East and South-South regions of Nigeria, amount to acts of terrorism and illegality is granted.

That an order proscribing the existence of the respondent (Indigenous People of Biafra) in any part of Nigeria, especially in the South-East and South-South regions of Nigeria, either in groups or as individuals, by whatever names they are called and publishing same in the official gazette and two national dailies is granted.

That an order restraining any person or group of persons from participating in any manner whatsoever in any form of activities involving or concerning the prosecution of the collective intention or otherwise of the respondent (Indigenous People of Biafra) under any other name or platform however called or described is granted.

The PUNCH quoted Malami, as saying in furtherance that IPOB stood proscribed as the court order had sanctioned the presidential approval of its proscription: It is true that IPOB was proscribed by the court today. It was the Federal High Court presided over by Justice Kafarati. The presidential approval proscribing the group has been sanctioned, confirmed, and affirmed by the court. The group stands proscribed.

Gazetting is the final stage and that takes an executive procedure, not legislative or judicial. As I have said, the executive aspect has been concluded by presidential approval and the judicial aspect has equally been concluded by the granting of the order by the court. That means the executive and the judicial processes have been concluded. It clearly remains the official gazetting which is the last thing to do.

The same report also quoted Lai Muhammed, then Minister of Information and Culture, arguably the most virulent megaphone of the former President and his government who upped the ante, as declaring that the matter was already sealed, with the most tangible accusation being that Kanu, was not only receiving money from foreign donors, but was actually soliciting funds to buy arms.

Here are his comments as recorded by the report:

We have the records, we know IPOB collects money from many people in [the] diaspora. They collect money from many people in Nigeria, they collect money from some foreign countries, this is clear.

Let me tell you, the financial headquarters is in France, we know. But you see, can you as a government stop people from sending money to their parents? You have to block the sources of finance; that is what I said recently. It is incontrovertible that some people in [the] diaspora contribute money to IPOB. Where does he get his money from? We know this as a fact.

Now, it is instructive that neither Malami, Muhammed, nor indeed anyone from that government cited anywhere either Kanu or any member of IPOB pulled an arrow, knifed, or shot a bullet at anyone which would have been quite ample and presented a perfect excuse for the onslaught waged against the supposed members in the manner the bloody campaign against them was carried out. That was the situation of the IPOB narrative at that stage before things went haywire and the group now became a symbol of insecurity in the South East.

Who would have forgotten that human carnage at the Head Bridge, Onitsha, where scores of youths armed with just Biafran flags were licentiously wasted by supposed security operatives? In fact, it is said that the offensive became so bad that the same operatives even combed hospitals around Onitsha and environs in search of survivors who were pulled out from hospital beds to finish the job before giving the victims a mass burial.

Who could have forgotten that gory scene in Aba? Like an act straight from a horror movie, scores of young men and women clapping hands and praying at a primary school in the city, were suddenly surrounded by supposed security operatives, and the next thing was, like practicing at a shooting range, their assailants knelt down, pointed their guns at the group, and opened fire on them?

For the inquisitive minds, who might wish to confirm the veracity of these events, videos of the grisly spectacles are all over the social media to date and available at the punch of buttons. In fact, at one of his outings in the US, Buhari was taken to task by Al Jazeera. In that interview, the female reporter who impressed it on him that the IPOB members were not armed, had opted to play the video of one of the scenes of the massacres, which the former President, promptly and vehemently declined to see.

Apart from videos of the killings, there were many others of youths being forced to roll in muddy ponds and swim in gutters while their tormentors in military gear who supervised the torture, watched with glee.

Mind you, many of these incidents happened before the declaration of the infamous *Operation Python Dance* by the military—that notorious programme seen in many quarters as the anti-climax of the brutality of the regime in the South East—that ill-famed operation that led to the storming of Kanu's Afarukwu home in Umuahia, the Abia State capital, resulting in his fleeing the country to increase the tempo of his IPOB campaigns from London.

Incidentally, and indeed, ironically, many Nigerians, including those from the South East, actually got to know about IPOB, Kanu or his Radio Biafra in London from these series of events, starting from his initial arrest on arrival in Nigeria on October 14, 2015, at the Golden Tulip Hotel, Airport Road, Lagos, where he was holed up after sneaking into the country.

Right or wrong, there is a groundswell of opinion elsewhere that if Buhari had ignored him as the previous governments did, particularly that of Goodluck Jonathan, his immediate predecessor,

Kanu and the IPOB issue, would have fizzled out or become as in-sipid and inconsequential as other self-styled, self-determination groups operating in parts of the country.

The argument became even more pointed in the face of the kid-glove treatment given to the Fulani herdsmen, a group which by then, had been declared by the Global Terrorist Index as the fourth deadliest terrorist group in the world by the same govern-ment, even after being linked to some of the most bestial and horrendous human carnages in history.

Of course, the counterarguments could be that it is only an un-responsive and irresponsible government that would ignore the national threat the group posed, especially given the utterances of its leader, Kanu, and more especially in the context of the Ni-gerian civil war history as a result of Biafra—the same position Buhari alluded to in that Al Jazeera interview.

But unassailable as it might seem, that argument becomes de-feated in the face of the selfsame President failing to treat the herdsmen in the same manner. Instead of going all out for them as in the case of IPOB, he began to offer himself as the official spokesman of the herdsmen, despite their own leaders making no similar pretences of inculpability in the onslaughts attributed to them.

For instance, at a meeting in the White House on Monday, April 30, 2018, Donald Trump, president of the United States, had con-fronted his Nigerian counterpart over the allegation of herdsmen killing Christians, a development which he said his country found unacceptable and intended to deal with.

Incidentally, Buhari gave the account of that encounter himself. *We have had very serious problems with Christians who are be-*

ing murdered in Nigeria. We are going to be working on that problem very, very hard because we cannot allow that to happen, his men quoted Trump as saying during a joint press briefing during the meeting.

But before then, the ex-POTUS was said to have challenged his visitor over the matter, privately. Again, Buhari himself narrated this encounter, while alone with Trump behind closed doors at the Oval Office. At a meeting with Ministers at a two-day ministerial performance review retreat held at the Presidential Villa, Abuja, on September 9, 2020, he said:

I believe I was about the only African among the less developed countries the President of [the] United States invited.

When I was in his office, only myself and himself—only God is my witness—he looked at me in the face, he asked, 'Why are you killing Christians?'

I wonder if you were the person how you will react. I hope what I was feeling inside did not betray my emotion so I told him that the problem between the cattle rearers and stagnant farmers I know is older than me, not to talk of him. I think I am a couple of years older than him.

With climate change and population growth and the culture of the cattle rearers, if you have 50 cows and they eat grass, any route to your water point, then they will follow it. It doesn't matter whose farm it is.

The First Republic set of leadership was the most responsible leadership we ever had. I asked the minister of agriculture to get a gazette of the early 60s which delineated the cattle route where they used meagre resources then to put earth dams, wind mills [and] even sanitary department.

So, any cattle rearer that allowed his cattle to go to somebody's farm would be arrested, taken before the court, the farmer would be called to submit his bill and if he couldn't pay, the cattle would be sold. But subsequent leaders, the VVIPs (very very important persons), encroached on the cattle routes. They took over the cattle rearing areas. So, I tried and explained to him (Trump) that this has got nothing to do with ethnicity or religion. It is a cultural thing.

You see what I mean? In the first place, the former President did not deny that there were such killings. His only explanation was that it was a cultural issue because the victims stood in the way of the herdsmen by closing the traditional cattle routes created by former Nigerian leaders to prevent conflicts.

He was to advance this position further. In an exclusive interview with *Arise News* crew in January 2021, where his visitors confronted him with a similar allegation, particularly one in which Samuel Ortom, then Governor of Benue State, pointedly accused him of giving official cover for the herdsmen, Buhari was no less forthcoming with a staunch defence of the group.

Here again was his reply:

The problem is trying to understand the culture of cattle rearers. There is a culture of the Fulanis. So, the government of Benue said I'm not disciplining the cattle rearers because I'm one of them. I cannot refuse to say I'm not one of them, but he's being very unfair to me and I told him that the Nigerian cattle rearers are not carrying anything more than a stick, sometimes a machete to cut trees and give to animals.

But those with sophisticated weapons with Ak-47 are from the Sahel area. They are Fulani people from Mauritania, Central Re-

*public Africa. They look the same so they will think they are Nige-
rians. But I assure you, we are trying to resuscitate these cattle
routes, grazing areas and make them accountable.*

Phew! This was the response of a President, the number one
citizen entrusted with the onerous duty of providing security and
welfare for the nationals, the sole function of government as en-
shrined in the constitution, to the mass slaughter of close to 100
souls in his country.

In fact, the Benue killings presented a tragi-comedy dimension.
At the heat of it all, Buhari had ordered Ibrahim Idris, then Inspector General of Police (IGP), to relocate to the place. But
no sooner did the police boss visit some locations in Makurdi,
the state capital, did he quickly leave and return back to Abuja.
Despite the hullabaloo that trailed his action and obvious disobedience, he never returned to the state. Yet, there were no
consequences, no punishments.

Buhari who gave the directive did nothing. In fact, when he reluc-
tantly visited the state after so much pressure from local and international interests, he feigned ignorance of the development.

*I'm not aware that the I-G did not spend 24 hours in the state as
directed by me. I am getting to know in this meeting,* he told a
bemused audience during the town hall meeting on March 12,
2018. The natural expectation would have been that now that
he had discovered, assuming, but not conceding that he did not
know, because the news of the IG abandoning his post was all
over the place, would have been instant punishment. But no!
Not even a slap on the wrist.

In fact, instead of sanctions, Idris would have been rewarded.
There were actually heavy speculations that the President was

actually toying with the idea of extending the tenure of the former IG, a development that met with a lot of pressure until he finally bowed and appointed Muhammed Adamu as his replacement in January 2019.

It is important to walk back this road to remind the unwary and even those who know, but prefer to pretend that IPOB is the hydra-headed monster eating babies from their mother's wombs, about its original parentage. I see the degeneration from its originally avowed non-violent posture into today's supposed killing machine and bastion of insecurity in the South East as more of a by-product from the venom of PMB, as he then was than the hot-air vituperations of MNK.

At worst, Kanu would not have ended up more than Ralph Uwazuruike of the Movement for the Actualisation of the Sovereign State of Biafra (MASSOB) or Ganiyu Adams of O'odua Peoples Congress (OPC), who are now big men in the society, having flown on the wings of die-hard supporters of ethnic identity. Mouthing Biafra through his IPOB, would obviously have catapulted him to an instant local hero and made him a billionaire like Uwazuirike or given him a status similar to Adams' Aare Ona kakanfo—such status of local ethnic champions and no more.

Is it not an uncanny piece of irony and contradiction in terms that El-Rufai, Mahdi, and even Buhari, from whose backyards dangerous groups known to have committed the most heinous crimes against society launch their offensives, including scorched-earth blitzkrieg in markets and public places, would now turn around and point in the direction of others whose activities constitute far fewer calamities?

Was that not the case Soyinka made so poignantly and pungently when on January 10, 2018, he practically spat fire again in that heart-warming interventionist epistle reminiscent of the straight-shooting, forthright, and fearless Kongi of global repute entitled: *Impunity rides again!*

Hear him:

It is happening all over again. History is repeating itself and alas within such an agonizingly short span of time. How often must we warn against the enervating lure of appeasement in the face of aggression and will to dominate! I do not hesitate to draw attention to Volume III of my INTERVENTION Series and to the chapter on The Unappeasable Price of Appeasement. There is little to add but it does appear that even the tragically fulfilled warnings of the past leave no impression on leadership not even when identical signs of impending cardiac arrest loom over the nation.

Boko Haram was still at that stage of putative probes when cries of alarm emerged. Then the fashion ideologues of society deployed their distancing turns of phrase to rationalize what were so obviously discernible as an agenda of ruthless fundamentalism and internal domination. Boko Haram was a product of social inequities they preached – one even chortled: We stand for justice so we are all Boko Haram! We warned that – yes indeed – the inequities of society were indeed part of the story but why do you close your eyes against other and more critical malfunctions of the human mind such as theocratic lunacy? Now it is happening again. The nation is being smothered in Vaseline when the diagnosis is so clearly – cancer!

We have been here before – now 'before' is back with a vengeance. President Goodluck Jonathan refused to accept that marauders had carried off the nation's daughters; President Mu-

hammadu Buhari and his government – including his Inspector-General of Police – in near identical denial appear to believe that killer herdsmen who strike again and again at will from one corner of the nation to the other are merely hot-tempered citizens whose scraps occasionally degenerate into "communal clashes" – I believe I have summarized him accurately. The marauders are naughty children who can be admonished paternalistically into good neighbourly conduct. Sometimes of course the killers were also said to be non-Nigerians after all. The contradictions are mind-boggling.

First the active policy of appeasement, then the language of endorsement. ElRufai, governor of Kaduna state, proudly announced that on assuming office he had raised a peace committee and successfully traced the herdsmen to locations outside Nigerian borders. He then made payments to them from state coffers to cure them of their homicidal urge which according to these herdsmen were reprisals for some ancient history and the loss of cattle through rustling. The public was up in arms against this astonishing revelation. I could only call to mind a statement by the same El Rufai after a prior election which led to a rampage in parts of the nation and cost even the lives of National Youth Service corpers. They were hunted down by aggrieved mobs and even states had to organize rescue missions for their citizens. Countering protests that the nation owed a special duty of protection to her youth, especially those who are co-opted to serve the nation in any capacity, El Rufai's comment then was: No life is more important than another. Today that statement needs to be adjusted to read perhaps – apologies to George Orwell: "All lives are equal but a cow's is more equal than others."

This seems to be the government view one that overtly or by implication is being amplified through act and pronouncement through clamorous absence by this administration. It appears to have infected even my good friend and highly capable minister, Audu Ogbeh, however insidiously. What else does one make of his statements in an interview where he generously lays the blame for ongoing killings everywhere but at the feet of the actual per-petrators! His words as carried by The Nation Newspapers:

"The inability of the government to pay attention to herdsmen and cow farming unlike other developed countries contributed to the killings." The Minister continued:

"Over the years, we have not done much to look seriously into the issue of livestock development in the country.... we may have done enough for the rice farmer, the cassava farmer, the maize farmer, the cocoa farmer but we haven't done enough for herds-men and that inability and omission on our part is resulting in the crisis we are witnessing today."

No, no, not so, Audu! It is true that I called upon the government a week ago to stop passing the buck over the petroleum situa-tion. I assure you, however, that I never intended that a reverse policy should lead to exonerating — or appearing to exonerate — mass killers, rapists, and economic saboteurs — saboteurs since their conduct subverts the efforts of others to economically secure their own existence, drives other producers off their land in fear and terror. This promises the same plague of starvation that afflicts zones of conflict all over this continent where liberally sown landmines prevent farmers from venturing near their prime source — the farm, often their only source of livelihood — and has created a whole population of amputees. At least those victims in Angola, Mozambique and other former war theatres mostly lived to tell the tale. These herdsmen, arrogant and unconscionable, have adopted a scorched-earth policy so that those other produc-ers – the cassava, cocoa, sorghum, rice, etc, farmers are brutally expelled from farm and dwelling.

Government neglect? You may not have intended it, but you made it sound like the full story. I applaud the plans of your minis-try, I am in a position to know that much thought – and practical steps – have gone into long term plans for bringing about the creation of 'ranches', 'colonies' – whatever the name – including the special cultivation of fodder for animal feed and so on and on. However, the present national outrage is over impunity. It rejects the right of any set of people, for whatever reason, to take arms against their fellow men and women, to acknowledge their exploits in boastful and justifying accents and in effect promise more of the same as long as their terms and demands are not met. In plain language, they have declared war against the na-tion and their weapon is undiluted terror. Why have they been permitted to become a menace to the rest of us? That is the is-sue!

Permit me to remind you that early in 2016, an even more hideous massacre was perpetrated by this same Murder Incor-porated – that is a numerical climax to what had been a series across a number of Middle Belt and neighbouring states with Benue taking the brunt of the butchery. A peace meeting was called, attended by the state government and security agencies of the nation including the Inspector General of Police. This group attended – according to reports- with AK47s and other weapons of mass intimidation visible under their garments. They were nei-ther disarmed nor turned back. They freely admitted the killings but justified them by claims that they had lost their cattle to the host community. It is important to emphasize that none of their spokesmen referred to any government neglect such as refusal to pay subsidy for their cows or failure to accord them the same facilities that had been extended to cassava or millet farmers. Such are the monstrous beginnings of the culture of impunity. We are reaping yet again the consequences of such tolerance of the intolerable. Yes, there indeed the government is culpable, definitely guilty of "looking the other way". Indeed, it must be held complicit.

This question is now current and justified: just when is terror? I am not aware that IPOB came anywhere close to this homicidal propensity and will to dominance before it was declared a terrorist organization. The international community rightly refused to go along with such an absurdity. For the avoidance of doubt, let me state right here and yet again that IPOB leadership is its own worst enemy. It repels public empathy; indeed I suspect that it deliberately cultivates an obnoxious image, especially among its internet mouthers who make rational discourse impossible. However, as we pointed out at the time, the conduct of that movement even at its most extreme could by no means be reckoned as terrorism. By contrast, how do we categorize Myeti? How do we assess a mental state that cannot distinguish between a stolen cow – which is always recoverable – and human life which is not. Villages have been depopulated far wider than those outside their operational zones can conceive. They swoop on sleeping settlements, kill and strut. They glory in their seeming supremacy. Cocoa farmers do not kill when there is a cocoa blight. Rice farmers, cassava and tomato farmers do not burn. The herdsmen cynically dredge up decades-old affronts – they did at the 2016 Benue "peace meeting" to justify the killings of innocents in the present – These crimes are treated like the norm. Once again, the nation is being massaged by specious rationalisations while the rampage intensifies and the spread spirals out of control. When we open the dailies tomorrow morning, there is certain to have been a new body count to be followed by the arrogant justification of the Myeti Allah.

The warnings pile up, the distress signals have turned into a prolonged howl of despair and rage. The answer is not to be found in pietistic appeals to victims to avoid 'hate language' and divisive attributions. The sustained killing monologue of the herdsmen is what is at issue. It must be curbed decisively and without further evasiveness.

Yes, Jonathan only saw 'ghosts' when Boko Haram was already excising swathes of territory from the nation space and abducting school pupils. The ghosts of Jonathan seem poised to haunt the tenure of Muhammadu Buhari.

The irony then is that Kongi, who wrote the above epistle, seems to have fallen into the same elaborately crafted, but obvious politically-induced IPOB he earlier questioned and rationalised their case. The question then is why the shift? What changed? Why is Peter Obi's political labour being labelled a Biafran agenda despite his best effort to make it a Nigerian thing? Why is Sunny Igboanugo being similarly painted? In short, why are all credible views, interventions, and or acts from everybody from the South East seen from the prism of Biafra and IPOB these days? Why is there not such tagging of other Nigerian citizens with similar and even provably deadlier groups?

Recall that Buhari was once appointed by Boko Haram as their chief negotiator with the Goodluck Jonathan government in the heat of their bloody campaign against Nigeria, including the abduction of the Chibok Girls. Yet, throughout his campaign for the presidency subsequently, this strange gesture never came into the fray fully. Why? Imagine, for instance, that it was Obi that was so appointed by IPOB to negotiate for them in such bizarre, but bloody adventure.

So, the question remains. Why Kongi? Surely it cannot be a function of ignorance. Especially coming from the trenches of NADECO, people like Soyinka should know better. This does not suggest that he does not know better. He was right there in the battlefield as one of the arrowheads of that historic struggle when even the normal scuffle at Oshodi Market, the stealing of a prayer mat in Abuja or the assault on a woman at Ogbete Market in Enugu, were attributed to NADECO by Abacha and his henchmen, baying for his blood and those of his colleagues in the struggle. Abraham Adesenya, the late NADECO leader, captured it all in that popular quip, where he indicated that if a man failed to impregnate his wife, the Abacha junta would blame it on NADECO.

It took the miraculous exit of Abacha from the scene for the haze to begin to clear and the true perspective of the patrons of insecurity of that era to start emerging—not as ghosts—and certainly not as NADECO members. Like NADECO was linked then to the failure of a man to impregnate his wife, similarly today IPOB is the reason the man was stung by a scorpion in the village of Amechi Awkunanaw, a boat capsized at Omambala River or a building collapsed at Eziama Obire.

Similarly, as it did not matter how outlandish the story sounded and how implausible the picture in NADECO days, it also does not seem to matter today with IPOB. So, on Monday, April 5, 2021, gunmen stormed the headquarters of the Imo State Police Command, destroyed part of it, and from there moved to the nearby Owerri Correctional Centre, released close to 2000 inmates, only for the same police to issue a statement a few hours later to blame it on IPOB.

It did not matter that this particular area was a high-level security zone, harbouring the headquarters of virtually all other security agencies operating in the state. Yet, the hoodlums were neither confronted nor rounded up and apprehended. Indeed, if anyone was ever arrested, prosecuted, and or convicted for that heinous crime, those concerned must have kept the information under wraps. All the public was left with, is the simple tag of IPOB.

Two weeks after, it was the same eerie story, this time at the Zone 13 Headquarters of the same Police at Ukpo, Dunukofia Local Government Area of Anambra State. Again, they operated freely, torched houses, vehicles, and other facilities in sight before disappearing. Arrest? Prosecution? Conviction?

Search me!

Then, it became more constant – Aguata Local Government headquarters, then Anaocha, then Ihiala, and many more – all in the same manner, same pattern, same modus operandi, and of course, same culprits – IPOB.

What about high-profile killings? Just like in the NADECO days, same pattern, same finger-pointing to one seemingly determined culprit. Ahmed Gulak, top APC chieftain in Owerri, Chike Akunyili, husband of the late Dora Akunyili of the NAFDAC fame in Onitsha, Oyibo Chukwu, Labour Party senatorial candidate in Enugu, Ogbonnaya Ugwu, top politician, five contractors abducted and murdered in Ebonyi.

Who has forgotten the image of those five bodies displayed by security operatives allegedly from a forest in Isikwuato Local Government of Abia State? They were said to be Hausa residents in the area killed by IPOB. That news broke on April 9, 2016. It is eight whole years now. Have the IPOB men, who supposedly committed that heinous crime been brought to book? Which court heard their case? Are they serving life sentences in any jail in Nigeria? Have they been hanged or faced a firing squad depending on the applicable laws? Which judge convicted them?

Is Kongi not supposed to be asking these questions that silently agitate the minds of right-thinking members of the society knowing what he knows? Up until the last weeks of the general election of 2023, facilities of the Independent National Electoral Commission (INEC), were still being attacked in the South East, sometimes with the perpetrators taking their time to rub their impunity in, in obvious mockery of their victims with such likely questions as – where are the security men you put your trust on? Let them come and save you!

What did he think of such horrible spectacles where these supposed IPOB members would have the temerity of, after making those videos of their attacks to these facilities, send them out through social media without traces or detection using modern facilities? Did he not see the editions where people conducting political events, were being molested – canopies pulled down, tables upturned, men and women forced on their bellies, some wantonly shot and killed point blank, cars, motorcycles, and other valuables found at the scenes, set ablaze in operations that sometimes last for hours without any response – all because the supposed IPOB did not want elections to hold in Igboland?

Instructively, till date, the official position of the IPOB, whose representatives have put faces to their names, is that the organisation is peaceful and non-violent. It is the position the group has maintained in all the allegations of being linked to the vicious and bloodthirsty UGM. It is their answer to being responsible for the bestiality, massacres, and other high crimes accompanying the enforcement of the weekly Monday Sit-at-home that has been operating in the South East. It is their response to being linked to the bombing of INEC facilities and public infrastructure anywhere and everywhere.

On the contrary, to prove differently to the right-thinking members of the public, with convincing, verifiable evidence, has remained the albatross of government. Surely, such a proof cannot be provided by just displaying bodies of supposed IPOB members purportedly felled in gun battles or by making a video of one young man in handcuffs or a group of men sitting on the floor 'confessing' to membership of IPOB. It cannot be because, someone is showing a video of a small hut in the bush, serving as a den where supposed IPOB members detain, torture, kill and even eat their victims. Certainly, those are stories, but not *The Story*. It takes far more than that.

Without prompt and effective arrest of perpetrators probably at the scene of crimes, with visible evidence to nail them in court and actual prosecution and sentencing, there is no way the government account will be convincing.

Yes! There is IPOB and there is IPOB. The question for a keen observer and a critical mind like WS, with adequate knowledge of the trajectory of events, must be, which IPOB? Is it IPOB that originally and consistently claims non-violence and projects itself as seeking for a referendum to determine where the people of the South East and any other groups or peoples they intend to co-opt into their fanciful idea of Biafra belong?

Or is it the NEW IPOB — the one derisively dismissed as an apparently contrived group of blood-thirsty felons and criminals — the IPOB even the likes of MNK have washed their hands of like Pontius Pilate and laboured to vehemently discountenance? Is it the IPOB that seems to have found a new taste for blood and like *Dracula*, enjoying its alluring feeling, goes into the streets to kill, maim, and destroy the same people it professes to defend their affairs, just to have more in a futile attempt to satiate its ravenous appetite?

Unfortunately, the atmosphere has since become more fluid with the absence of Kanu who has remained in detention since June 2021, making the IPOB situation more uncertain, difficult, and complicated. This fluidity has remained more apparent in the orders and counter-orders, claims and counterclaims over the sit-at-home phenomenon.

In fact, the sit-at-home fuss, visibly points to the intrigues and manipulations of IPOB as a means of destabilisation by forces outside the control of MNK and his group, just like the emergence of Simon Ekpa on the scene, gives impetus to the suspicion therein that what the world is seeing in the South East is akin to the biblical hand of Esau and voice of Jacob.

On countless occasions, Emma Powerful, official spokesman of IPOB, as well as Ifeanyi Ejiofor, lawyer to Kanu, have sworn that Ekpa, who claims to be the new leader in the absence of Kanu, was not speaking for the IPOB, especially in his numerous sit-at-home declarations. Yet the orders of the Finland-based Ekpa, have always carried the force of power. Even keen observers would have lost count of the number of people killed as victims of the supposed disobedience of these orders – whole vehicles set ablaze with passengers inside them, others pulled out and shot, many pulled out of their business premises and killed.

On October 9, 2022, Powerful in another strident effort to distance IPOB from Ekpa, wrote:

We the global movement and family of the Indigenous People of Biafra IPOB led and commanded by Onyendu, Mazi Nnamdi Kanu is very much aware that the Nigeria Government is, directly and indirectly, sponsoring election violence in Biafra land with the intention to internationally blackmail the Indigenous People of Biafra IPOB as an anti-democratic group.

The IPOB leadership has for the umpteenth time stated unequivocally that part of our modus operandi in our agitation for freedom has never been, is not, and will not be violent agitation.

This explains our consistent demand for the UN to organise a Referendum in the Biafran territory for the Biafran people to determine their destiny. To this effect, IPOB is neither contemplating nor will it encourage or sponsor anyone or group to disrupt Nigeria's shambolic selection process called an election.

IPOB has constantly made it public that we have no interest in and cannot legitimise the aberration they call an election in Nigeria. We are a focused, determined, and disciplined freedom-fighting movement, not political thugs.

IPOB is devoted to the cause of liberating our people from subjugation and from modern-day slavery and Neo-colonialism and will not allow ourselves to be distracted from this very objective.

The world must hold to account the Nigeria Government and the criminals it is covertly recruiting and positioning in the South East to create an environment of violence and after causing the violence will turn around to blame IPOB.

IPOB is not part of Nigeria's sham election and will never be part of it. IPOB is solely focused on Biafra Independence struggle which Nigeria Government and its allies are working very hard to derail with their daily propaganda and blackmail against Mazi Nnamdi Kanu and IPOB members worldwide.

Our demands are simple: the unconditional release of our leader, Mazi Nnamdi Okwuchukwu Kanu, fix a date for a referendum for Biafrans to decide their fate either for freedom or for a Sovereign Biafran Nation or for permanent subjugation and oppression in the Republic of Nigeria.

As we have said in our previous press statement, the Nigeria government and its compromised security agencies are responsible for most criminal activities going on in Biafraland and some other parts of Nigeria. This very fact has been confirmed by Nigeria Army officers in their letter to the Presidency.

Ifeanyi Ejiofor, Kanu's lawyer, was even more frontal. Emerging from a visit to the IPOB leader at the facility of the Department of State Services (DSS) in Abuja, where he had been in detention, he said Kanu was not only aware of the parlous situation in the South East, but also clear about the role of Ekpa as a government agent: He wrote:

We visited our indefatigable and formidable Client – Onyendu Mazi Nnamdi Kanu today being the 31st Day of July 2023 at the SSS Headquarters, Abuja, where he is still being illegally and unconstitutionally held in solitary confinement.

Today's visit was to brief Onyendu on pertinent developments *concerning his specific written order calling off the senseless sit-at-home hitherto being enforced by enemies of our people.*

Onyendu used the opportunity provided by the visit to remind our people and all Ezigbo Umuchineke to note that whoever still goes about to observe any unauthorized sit-at-home directive should know that he or she is working for the Nigerian Government to destroy our once peaceful land. Onyendu was very emphatic that Simon Ekpa is procured and fully bankrolled by the Nigerian Government to cause unrest in our region.

Even Kanu himself, was no less emphatic when he had the opportunity to speak on the matter during his appearance in court. The IPOB leader, who spoke partly in Igbo claiming that he was not happy with what he was hearing, said: My heart is troubled. Anyone that engages in kidnapping, killing people. Listen to me, anybody who is involved in stealing, kidnapping, and engaging in deceit is a thief. We are here to fight for freedom, for equity and fairness. That is what we're fighting for, nothing more, nothing less. And we cannot be cowed by anybody. We're without fear of our enemies. We will speak the truth always.

I want the journalists here today to go and ask the government of Nigeria, what happened to treasonable felony? Where are those charges today? They've just disappeared because they have no evidence against me. Anybody committing crimes cannot go scot-free. I swear it. They cannot go scot-free. Anybody that is involved in crimes in the East cannot go scot-free. They're doing this because I'm in DSS.

If I'm outside, nobody can try this kind of rubbish. They know it very well. And I suspect that some people in government are complicit and making money with insecurity. They're making money with it. They know that if Nnamdi Kanu is outside, in two minutes this nonsense will stop. Who is that idiot? Who is the bagger that will speak when I'm talking? Who is the fool? Who is the idiot I ask that I'll give orders in the East and anybody will counter it? Who is the bastard I'm asking you?

Nobody can! Am I not Nnamdi Kanu! Who is the idiot? Anybody involved in any form of violence or insecurity in the South East in the name of IPOB is a goner and they know it. Let me come out of this nonsense, this mess, and two minutes only – only two minutes I guarantee you there will be peace in the South East, not only in the South East, everywhere in the East if not the entire South.

So, with these series of denials, who then is Ekpa and his group representing? This ought to be the abiding question. There is even a third leg – the Asari Dokubo angle. Until recently, nobody knew that he actually had any hand in the South East security situation. That was until he confessed in June last year that he actually had a security contract with Buhari and South East was one of the areas he claimed the pact covered.

Till date, the details of this security job he did in the zone as captured in that controversial interview inside the Presidential Villa after visiting President Bola Tinubu, have not been made public. Is it not important for Nigerians to ask and to know, especially when he also revealed in that outing, where he took on the Nigerian military, to having a private military company?

In fact, he also boasted that his men were actually better than Nigerian soldiers and to underscore this claim, he put them on display in another video some days after the Villa visit. Now what role did those men play? What specific briefs did Asari get from

Buhari and what were the contract terms, especially with the South East and more specifically with IPOB?

Recall that this was the same Asari who had, after revealing that he was of an Igbo parentage and therefore an Igbo man, and swearing with the names of all the Kalabari gods towards the Biafran project, teamed up with Kanu to use IPOB as the vehicle to bring it about. At what time and in what circumstances did he change his mind? At what point did he do a rethink?

Surprisingly, the former Niger Delta militant not only fell out a few months later with Kanu, but so strong was the hostility therefrom that he swore to eliminate the IPOB leader. Yet even at this point, he still did not abandon the Biafran project. In fact, on March 14 he went ahead to announce what he called the Biafran Customary Government (BCG).

Here was his statement as released by one Law Mefor, spokesman for the said BCG:

We as people have resolved that as Biafra, it's time for us to take our destiny in our hands and bring freedom to ourselves and our children and the generation of Biafrans yet unborn. I hesitate a little but I thank God that it's time for us to do our duty and our service to the motherland I have accepted this role. I have dedicated my life hundred percent to play this role.

My first act today in taking this position is to name those who would be on the driver's seat to navigate through this period of tempest, this period of uncertainty with me. I want to call on our brother George Onyibe to come on board to join as the secretary of the defacto customary government of the State of Biafra. He will take care of the administrative day-to-day administration of the Biafra State.

I also call on our brother Emeka Emeka Esiri to take care of the legal needs of this nascent government. My brothers and sisters the four of us will kick start the process, others will come on board. We want volunteers who are committed we want volunteers because there is nothing anymore. We are the people who have volunteered to salvage ourselves and the rest of us.

I also call on Biafrans in the various provinces of the Biafra nations in Aba, Abakiliki, Anang, Awka, Calabar, Degema, Eket, Enough, Nsukka, Ogoja, Oji River, Okigwe, Onitsha, Opobo, Orlu, Owerri, Port Harcourt, Umuahia, Uyo and Yenagoa provinces. We are going to proceed to set up provincial structures of government starting with provincial assemblies and provincial governance and administrators.

Nobody can stop us. Nobody can blockade us as they did in the first war. We're not going to fight any war with anybody we're walking to freedom. We will not shoot any gun with them they will prepare their weapon but they will have nobody to kill with their weapon.

Now listen to the same Asari and mark his words as he turned 360 degrees, some months after. In a video he released on Thursday, July 6, 2023, he not only lampooned the same Igbo, he professed to have as his root, but the manner he spoke about the Biafran idea suggested that it was probably his ghost that was practically spitting fire a few months back.

Hear him:

Please in the name of God why do we allow this vicious cycle of irritation of people who claim to be victims when they are the oppressors and the people offending others? Let the Igbo go so that there will be enough resources for other people to manage.

They don't even need a referendum. The President and National Assembly should meet and someone courageous enough should sponsor a bill at the National Assembly. There should be a constitutional amendment. The five Igbo states and any group of people who want to join them should go.

Surprise? No! Gutted should be the right word. This was a man who claimed less than two years earlier to be Igbo. This was the same man who swore to lead the agitation for the creation of Biafra to the extent of forming a government in that regard to boot.

But this is all there is to it. IPOB – their IPOB- and Biafra, their Biafra, becoming in the main, a manipulative tool used to achieve predetermined agendas. What other element could have given Buhari the platform, leeway, and excuse to unleash his venom on a people he described as a dot in a circle? How else could he have found a fertile ground to demonstrate his infamous 95-5 per cent political project against Ndigbo, which became emblematic of his government with regards to the treatment of Ndigbo throughout the duration of his miserable eight years?

Ideally, nobody would exculpate Kanu and his group from the whole sad story. For one, he was the originator, promoter, and patron of this brand of Biafran agitation that IPOB represented. Nobody could remove him from the effect of his combustive, combative declarations. But that certainly could not be a reason to bespatter the entire Igbo people with the same paintbrush. Why was nobody linking Atiku Abubakar and Rabiu Kwankwaso, who also ran in the same election with Boko Haram, Islamic State of West African Province (ISWAP), globally acknowledged as terrorist organisations, or the Fulani herdsmen officially designated the fourth deadliest group in the world?

Why was nobody associating Tinubu with the activities of Sunday Igboho or Banji Akintoye of the Yoruba Nation leadership – groups with no marked difference from Nnamdi Kanu's IPOB in both the contents of their message and comburant declarations? Why did Kadiria Ahmed not ask Atiku, who also appeared on her programme, to condemn Boko Haram or Fulani herdsmen as she demanded of Obi?

Even Buhari, did anyone ever try to pin the activities of Boko Haram on him? Again, do not forget that the group, prior to the 2015 presidential election, appointed him as their official front during the negotiation for the release of the Chibok Girls hostages. Yet all these were brushed aside and he became President. Even with the Fulani herdsmen completing their task of entrenching their faces and stamping their authority in the polity as untouchables.

Even with such high-profile events as kidnapping of Olu Falae in his farm at Ilado village in Akure North Local Government Area of Ondo State or the killing of Funke Olakunri, daughter of Reuben Fasoranti, leader of the pan-Yoruba socio-political group Afenifere, Buhari, a known Fulani with manifest love for his people, never lost his subsequent re-election in 2019 regardless of his ethnic profile.

So, why must Obi take the tag of IPOB and Biafra at every turn even when he made a clear declaration to the entire world – *don't vote for me because of my ethnic or religious background, vote for me because I'm a Nigerian?* Which of the other candidates that contested the 2023 presidential election was that confident to make such an instructive declaration?

Simple answer! IPOB, their IPOB, has since become a special

purpose vehicle (SPV) to prosecute all manner of anti-Igbo projects. With that, Buhari could continue his unfinished war with the Igbo. Remember, the wife Aisha once told a gathering of the wives of military and police officers that he suffered from post-traumatic stress disorder (PTSD), by fighting in the civil war as a young officer.

Remember that viral video also where Femi Fani-Kayode revealed the content of their private meeting where he reportedly told him that he would never forgive Ndigbo because they killed Northern leaders. It does not seem to matter that for reasons of what is supposed to be a purely military affair, millions of the same Igbo had been killed in the pogrom that followed the civil war and many other civil unrests.

Today, after posting the most woeful record in Nigerian governance history, the only success that he would wear as a badge of honour is the abduction of Kanu from Kenya and his subsequent incarceration, a project he must have invested all his military skills and Nigerian resources into pulling through. Under him, Boko Haram not only festered but gave birth to other insurgents, who upped the ante, sacking communities, abducting school children, even breaking fortified Kuje Prison gates and escaping.

In the same manner, Mahdi, El-Rufai, et al, also tried to use the same SPV to scare away Nigerians, especially in the North, from voting Obi, Soyinka's recourse to IPOB in reference to Obi is only diversionary. In other words, our revered Nobel Laureate is employing the same tactics, not only to mitigate the impact of what could pass as the worst election in the history of Nigeria but to shine the image of the beneficiary. That he would tread that route is the tragedy of the story.

DATTI-AHMED: THE INJURED AS THE SCAPEGOAT

Let me confess once more that I am struggling to capture fully or comprehend totally the language employed in *Baiting Igbo-phobia: The Sunny Igboanugo Thesis*. Like every WS book I have read, I had to go the extra mile of getting some interpretations. I am told that you must attain some intellectual level or acquire some literary skills to understand Soyinka – that only then would you join the special club that enjoy his writing. Well, from the outset I have neither attained both nor struggling to. I am very comfortable in my comfort zone where, like every simpleton, I go for the basics. Such elevated language does not appeal to my literary palate.

Even Kongi himself has done me the favour in this regard by acknowledging that I am not playing in his class. Let me add that I am not even aiming at scratching the shoes of that class, not to talk of dreaming of joining it. I have to state this from the outset, lest I veer off completely from the intent of his intervention as it concerns me and be blamed for it. The wordings are too heavy for me and to a large extent, quite confusing.

Therefore, let it be known that what I am trying to employ here is what a popular thief in my village called *ntam nta anya*. Let me explain. Not lettered as virtually all his colleagues in that trade during his time, he confessed that it was through the application of *ntam nta anya* – what in our Ajegunle street language we referred to as *one kain eye* or *corner-corner eye* that he got to know that *catch am* meant *apprehend him* – so that whenever he heard those words, he was prepared to greet the ground with his heels.

Bereft of the skills to read and understand Soyinka and only using the technique of *ntam nta anya* as my guide, I again proceed to distil some of the basic issues in his *Baiting Igbophobia: The Sunny Igboanugo Thesis*. Let me address, for instance, his insistence that the infamous interview Yusuf Datti Baba-Ahmed granted to Channels Television, was in preparation for an impending apocalypse. I disagreed then when he first toed that line, and I disagree today that there was any basis to come to such a damning and alarmist projection. I insist that Kongi's interpretation, was mere propaganda, deliberately so, to boot.

Perhaps a recap. On April 5, 2023, the sage in an interview with Arise News, Nigeria's A-list television network, had said:

I have never heard anyone threaten the judiciary on television the way Datti did. I heard the kind of menacing, blackmailing language as that to which we were treated by Datti. That kind of do-or-die attitude and prAovocation is not what I think we have all been struggling for.

Nearly the totality of Datti's comment in the interview was unbecoming. It was like trying to dictate to the supreme arbiter of the nation and whatever you think of the Supreme Court, it is an institution we all refer to sooner or later. But Datti kept saying in his wisdom that the Supreme Court must agree with me. That is what is known as fascistic language and it is not acceptable.

It was like a thunderbolt! Throughout the run of the 2023 presidential election and following the actions and activities of political gladiators and their goons, some of which threatened the very foundation of Nigeria, not a few people wondered about the deafening silence of Wole Soyinka, one of the few remaining consciences of Nigeria. This is his turf – the moment when he usually roared like the lion, forcing the ground to quake to its foundation and the deaf to listen, one of which was in the run to the 2015 elections. Why the silence? Were all well with the Kongi? The questions were asked silently and loudly.

So, coming out with these comments, and in the manner he did, practically left not a few Nigerians in shock. But immediately that initial reaction of shock ended and the haze cleared, especially when it became obvious from where he was coming and on which side of the divide he was, the next natural reaction was outrage – in torrents and from various quarters. No doubt, Kongi was and still is a deity in Nigeria, metaphorically and in real terms. But deities are not expected to overstretch their relevance. For even the obeisance to them must have limits. Hence the local parlance that a deity, which overreaches itself, is shown the wood from which it was carved.

In the Nigeria of that particular era – the 2023 presidential election mood – there was no room for a middle-ground. It was an either-or – them and us – oppressors and the oppressed stratification. So, by those comments via Arise Television interview of Wednesday, April 5, 2023, Soyinka clearly made his choice – one that was very clear to Nigerians. The avalanche of reactions that followed was not only natural but expected.

If there was any surprise in the entire sequence, it was in the expectation of the sage that he would come out of that outing smelling roses as he used to. He must have been heavily disappointed that he did not get the cheers and accolades his previous interventions drew. That he could have expected a different outcome, really underscored how much he had taken Nigerians for granted.

In fact, nobody seemed to realise that there was a second leg to the interview in which the Nobel Laureate was complaining about some people parroting fake news about him and even offered a reward of $1,000 for anyone that could lead him to those involved. In the entire bedlam of hard words that trailed the outing, few people actually referred to the anger of the Kongi to the so-called fake news peddlers:

Please beware of fake news. A lot of damage is being done by fake news. Even as recently as a few days ago. Some garbage, verbiage, nauseating and praise-singing tracts, which we have seen so many times before, have been resurrected and attributed to Wole Soyinka. It makes me sick. If people want to be praise singers, let them do it in their own father's name and leave Soyinka out of it. I want to use this opportunity to announce a reward of $1000 to anyone who can finger successfully the author of some of the tracts which have been attributed to me over the past six months," he had stated.

It is difficult ascertaining if anyone actually went in search of the culprits he complained about. Even if Kongi paid out his $1,000, it must have been swallowed up in the cacophony of voices arising as a consequence of his stance on the election. Perhaps he would have thought the sound of dollars, a magic word in Nigeria, would have sent people into the street in search of the fake news urchins. If indeed that was his intention, he probably would have realised that at certain times the lure of the greenback, could actually take a back seat.

In fact, by that strange position on the election and the commentary thereof, he could have been that irascibly naughty boy, who on his way back from school, saw a hive of wasps hanging on a tree-branch and instead of fleeing from it, decided to test the potency of its stings by throwing a stone into its midst. The consequences were as swift as they were grave, causing the Kongi to dodge and duck under the cushion of ornamental words, in an attempt to try save his skin, a futile effort, if you asked me.

Of course, it was not the first time Kongi squared up with Nigerian youths. His testy times with them over the American Green Card issue should have warned him that times were evolving. How? Why? Soyinka had, in the run to the 2016 US presidential election, vowed to tear his Green Card should Americans vote Donald Trump. However, when it came to pass, instead of cutting this vital document to pieces, Kongi started changing his words, or so it appeared. Naturally, he was taken to task as expected in today's internet world, which never forgets.

That was actually the genesis of his war with today's internet community, which the sage has used almost all the words in his rich vocabulary to denigrate and demonise. Only that what he faced this time, in the election palaver, became a child's play from that episode.

The former could be likened to the *Rumble in the Jungle* where a Muhammad Ali squared up with George Foreman in the ring amid cheering spectators. This time, it was the real war with different spectators flinching at each impact – like the Baghdad blitzkrieg, in which the US tested some of its latest weapons to smoke out Saddam Hussein or its replication in Libya against Muammer Ghadaffi.

If in the Green Card saga, they had come with truckloads, this time they came with train coaches, cargo planes, and shiploads to drop their contents at the doorsteps of the revered sage. So much were the bombardments that Kongi had to in split-seconds duck behind his fortress – words!

So, on April 7, 48 hours after his Arise News appearance, he returned fire through a usually well-articulated epistle – the way only he could demonstrate – evidence that he neither picked his Nobel Laureate status from the streets of Abeokuta nor bought it from Dugbe Market. It was an epistle that showcased his mastery of the language and how to apply it to his purpose, strung so delicately like a weaverbird.

Entitled: *Fascism on course* he wrote:

It would appear that a record discharge of toxic sludge from our notorious smut factory is currently clogging the streets and sewers of the Republic of Liars. It goes to prove the point that provoked the avalanche EXACTLY! The seeds of incipient fascism in the political arena have evidently matured. A climate of fear is being generated. The refusal to entertain corrective criticism, even differing perspectives of the same position, has become a badge of honour and certificate of commitment. What is at stake ultimately is – Truth, and at a most elementary level of social regulation: when you are party to a conflict, you do not attempt to intimidate the arbiter, attempt to dictate the outcome, or impugn without credible cause his or her neutrality, even before hearing has commenced. That is a ground rule of just proceeding. Short of this, Truth remains permanently elusive.

The ensuing cacophony has been truly bewildering. It strikes me as a possible ploy to smother recent provocations by other far more trenchant issues such as the revelation of declarations of a religious war. If so, let it be known that I have long declared war against religious fundamentalism, the nature of which justifies the butchery, kidnapping, and enslavement of students in the name of religion. That aspirant's alleged gaffe cuts no ice with me. Far more alarming was the grotesque fantasy of the Chief Justice of the Supreme Court disguised on a wheelchair, zooming off in space to a secret meeting with other parties to the conflict. On its own, that is sufficiently scary. Swiftly followed thereafter by a television tirade of intimidation, it strikes one as more than the mere antics of the mentally deranged. The tactics are familiar: ridicule, incriminate, then intimidate. Objective: undermine the structure of justice. Just as a reminder: I was not being rhetorical when I declared on exiting prison detention: Justice is the first condition of humanity.

The instigating contest — Nigerian Democracy 2023 — has witnessed much that is innovative — largely in the retrogressive vein. Violence and ethnic profiling. "Spiritual" warfare in the shape of sacrificial rams to keep "disloyal" communities under restraint — in short, intimidation yet again! Easily overlooked, however, are those missives of violence directed against dissenting voices, real or suspect. Such, for instance, were the virulent attacks and threats to the musician Seun Kuti, his family, and iconic music Shrine. His crime consisted of nothing more than declaring the name "Obidient" derogatory to his sense of civic dignity and activist history. Such beginnings – and instances are numerous – have culminated in the open intimidation of the Court of Last Resort even before proceedings have begun. By the way, I do agree with Seun Kuti; 'Obidients' is one of the most repulsive, off-putting concoctions I ever encountered in any political arena. Some love it, however, and this is what freedom is about. Choice. Taste. Free emotions. By contrast, I have no quarrel with "Yes Daddy". Roman Catholics are used to saying "Yes Father". Secularists say "Enh Baba". The context and content are what matters and lies – where established – raise bothersome issues such as Integrity Deficiency.

Let us remind ourselves of the following: In any adjudication, society finds it unacceptable that a party to the dispute resorts to influencing tactics by extra-judicial means – such as bribery. Intimidation and threats are merely the obverse complements of material inducement. Those who fail to appreciate this are entirely free to their existence in an illusory world.

We shall add the following pointer for this particular electoral tussle – the news may be unpleasant, but here it comes. Quite a few pundits have set out in some impressive – not necessarily persuasive – detail the possibility that the complainants in this presidential election are not as strongly planted on the victory podium as they presume, see – for instance – Ambassador Haastrup's fascinating analysis in Newspeak etc. of 6 April. Right or wrong? That is not the issue. What the nation needs to know right now is if you are planning to send assassins after such negative analysts! Coming to terms with an unpalatable projected eventuality – sorry – possible eventuality counsels deep reflection, not demonisation of the bearer of sour news. For the seriously committed, it requires pulling back the horns a little in order to regroup, rethink, and resurge. Democracy is sometimes a long haul. Some of us have been at it for quite a while.

I am well aware that the foregoing is further invitation for more nauseous bilge from the besotted. Please be my guest. It is, after all, one of those special seasons of convergence of two seasons of self-flagellation. Fasting makes bearers of constricted minds even more light-headed. Delusions fill the vacuum.

Oh yes, could these rabid parochial minds of easy excitation also kindly stop flattering themselves that one's energies are consecrated solely to the nation space known as Nigeria? The whines of "silence" are relative to the reading scope and world knowledge of idle complainants as well as their grasp of the chain of continuity. I choose my methods of intervention without the permission of social media border patrols, so where you find a gap, just pick up the baton where last deposited and stop whining and belly-aching — "he stopped talking all this while, why now?" etc. etc. ad nauseum. Flat, easy disposable lies that gain traction by repetition. However, even more importantly, they remain irrelevant to the rights and wrongs of ongoing material issues. Sadly, these virtue vigilantes succeed with the ignorant and susceptible — especially among the younger, confused generation. The consequence is that the nation is plagued by fake CVs compiled by all kinds of amateur commentators still wet behind the ears who have too few truths to build on before they are corralled into positions of No-Retreat. Nowhere has this been more evident than in the effrontery of attempts to place the present contention on the same podium as the twenty-year old anti-Abacha struggle! This gross abuse of historic licence actually provides smug satisfaction for rookie activists. I advise them to seek out the school of survivors where pertinent lessons still exist for those with sufficient *humility to LEARN before MOUTHING! Otherwise, their world of false mythologies will collapse under their feet and leave them dangling in the void.*

May I seize this opportunity, by the way, to condemn the sanctions imposed on Channels Television, which anchored the performance of the LP candidate. As stated, I watched the programme keenly – saw the valiant efforts of the interviewer to ensure fair hearing. I fail to understand just where the station could be faulted, except from a disposition for injustice. To sustain that penalty is to give joy to others who turn the Internet into a soakaway for their rancid emissions yet feel that others should be silenced. If Channels feels up to it, I offer myself, willing to engage Mr Datti – or any nominee of his – on its platform on this very bone of contention – one-on-one – without the malodorous intervention of media trolls and with the same interviewer as mediator. That should be taken as a serious offer.

Project Nigeria, I must confess, has become near terminally soul-searing. Do I still believe in it? I am no longer certain but – first, we must rid ourselves of the tyranny of the ignorant and the opportunism of time-servers. In any case, there is not much else to engage one on a foundation of ownership stakes. There is, of course, always the possibility of a Revolution with a clarity of purpose and acceptance of all attendant risks, including costly errors. Revolutions are not, however, based on the impetus of speculative power entitlement. No matter, until that moment, the structures that ensure just and equitable cohabitation must be protected from partisan appropriation – be it from material inducement, fake news, or verbal terrorism – the last being the contribution of one who is positioned to assume co-leadership of the nation, no less. Revolution is not about lining up behind the nearest available symbol. When a symbol does emerge, however, we are still obliged to examine every aspect of what is fortuitously on offer and continue to guard our freedoms every inch of the way.

Before I take myself off for – well, next port of call – the final word goes to a favourite maverick propagated, even as he matched his words by action. I suspect that in this instance, we find ourselves on opposite sides of the strategic fence – that is democracy. This now coopted watchword of his formulation remains apt, applicable to all who strive for authentic social transformation: **Your mumu don do!**

Ramadan Kareem. Happy Easter!

Indeed, I had thought that Kongi would have at least mitigated his words, if not shifted his position after his objective or what I thought was his objective, had since been achieved. But in the *Baiting Igbophobia: The Sunny Igboanugo Thesis*, he seemed adamant that he was and still is right. I find it funny when he wrote in the book: *That party sent out an impassioned demagogue – but of the stature, no less, of a university proprietor – in the person of its presidential running mate. Our democratic role model went on air and threatened to bring down the entire national edifice unless its own ruling on the contest was adopted. Scatter the pieces on the board, walk off, and unilaterally proclaim Foul Play!*

Of course, he was referring to Datti Baba-Ahmed, Obi's running mate. I have since returned to that interview in reference and watched it for the hundredth time perhaps to see where Soyinka's high-sounding accusations – tapering towards insurrections or outright war – derived. For emphasis, these were Datti-Ahmed's exact words:

We came third according to the result released by INEC. In reality, we came first. Nigeria is in a state of constitutional crisis and we are not realising that yet. A certificate of return has been issued to a so-called President-elect unconstitutionally. There are therefore two understandings of the declaration made. One is the one by INEC and the other is the one of the people. Anybody can read section 134 and take a position. We are entitled to our view of the crisis facing Nigeria now.

The certificate of return issued to Tinubu is a dud certificate. Therefore, the requirement to be declared as president-elect has not been met by Tinubu/Shettima ticket. So, for people who understand Section 134, there is really no president-elect.

Section 134 stipulates who to be declared and issued certificate of return. It is only that candidate that has scored the highest number of votes and at least 25 per cent in 2/3 of the states of the federation and the Federal Capital Territory.

It is very clear Tinubu does not have 25 per cent in the FCT; we denied him. We got 61 per cent. Atiku does not have 25 per cent. We denied both of them. So, by the Nigerian constitution, which must not be bridged, Tinubu does not satisfy the constitution to be declared president-elect. So, there is no president-elect for Nigeria now because the declared one violates the constitution of the Federal Republic of Nigeria.

The way they are going, disregarding the call of the people, violating the constitution, even if they swear in Tinubu and Shettima, they are swearing in an unconstitutional government. That is my interpretation and that is indeed a correct interpretation.

You cannot swear [in] people who have not met the constitutional requirements; you can't do that. If you do it, you have done something unlawful, something unconstitutional. I'm not taking risks with my safety and with my life. It was more extreme for [INEC Chairman Mahmood] Yakubu to issue that certificate; it was reckless. He's putting all our lives in danger.

Did Baba-Ahmed speak out of turn? I did not and still do not think so, especially given his proviso that it was how he understood Section 134 (2) of the 1999 Constitution which says:

"A candidate for an election to the office of President shall be deemed to have been duly elected where, there being more than two candidates for the election: (a) he has the highest number of votes cast at the election; and (b) he has not less than one-quarter of the votes cast at the election in each of at least two-thirds of all the States in the Federation and the Federal Capital Territory, Abuja."

Now compare this with the *Iya Chukwudi* video, with which Igbo people in Lagos were warned to stay away from the governorship election that came two weeks after the February 25 presidential exercise, if they were not willing to vote for the APC. That video was shared and received by virtually every Nigerian that had a mobile phone.

"We have begged them. If they don't want to vote for us, it is not a fight. Tell them, Mama Chukwudi, if you don't want to vote for us, sit down at home. Sit down at home," were the exact and operative words one *MC Oluomo,* real name Musiliu Akinsaya, who made the threat, used to drive home the message. That open threat by the former Chairman of the Lagos State branch of the National Union of Road Transport Workers (NURTW), then Chairman of the Lagos State Park Management Committee (PMC), was made just hours apart from Datti Baba-Ahmed's supposed

fascist statement that got Soyinka so rankled.

Yes! The police excused the comment calling it "a joke" after the selfsame MC Oluomo, who made it recanted, saying he was only joking with one Mama Chukwudi selling noodles and other fast foods at a certain motor park. Perhaps this later-day repudiation would have been compelling if the same man had not been seen in an earlier video practically harassing the same Igbo people.

Yes! Another video captured him on the day of the presidential election telling those who were not voting APC to leave one of the polling station venues he stormed with his henchmen. That evidence was also very much in the public domain. Was that physical harassment also a joke as they would have Nigerians believe?

Even beyond that, were many Igbo people not victims of the violent attacks by hoodlums who ostensibly took a cue from that warning by the PMC boss to perpetrate mayhem? Was that also a joke? Between that and the mere words spoken on television by an aggrieved Datti Baba-Ahmed, which was more dangerous to democracy and which was more threatening to Nigeria?

Trust Nigerians! They pointed it out to WS that the monster he saw emerging from the sea, for which he was sounding the village war drums to summon the warriors to arms, was no more than a phantom figure, one which not only his eyes could see but probably less capable of causing any harm than the tiny nails of the lizard on the trunk of a tree. They told him that ignoring the real danger and focusing on this imaginary fiend, was not only a crime, but *The Crime*.

In his April 7 epistle, Kongi had, apart from declaring that his attention was divided beyond Nigerian shores, indicated that he could pick and choose which issues to respond to and the one to ignore with these words:

Oh yes, could these rabid parochial minds of easy excitation also kindly stop flattering themselves that one's energies are consecrated solely to the nation space known as Nigeria? The whines of "silence" are relative to the reading scope and world knowledge of idle complainants as well as their grasp of the chain of continuity. I choose my methods of intervention without the permission of social media border patrols, so where you find a gap, just pick up the baton where last deposited and stop whining and belly-aching – "he stopped talking all this while, why now?" etc. etc. ad nauseum. Flat, easy disposable lies that gain traction by repetition."

That was where our respected sage missed the point and the young men and women minced no words in telling him so when in chorus they seemed to echo:

Wrong Sir! You do not cherry-pick on national matters. Not anymore! Certainly not the route you are taking. You have grown beyond enjoying privacy not because it is not your right to so do but because you are Wole Soyinka – literary icon, Africa's first and only Nobel Laureate in Literature and one of the total 28 winners in the continent, freedom fighter, democratic crusader and above all – indisputable conscience of the nation.

In other words, it means that Kongi's opinion on any and every matter in Nigeria counts. It counted yesterday, it counts today, it will count tomorrow and might even count in the generations to come. So, for him to throw a bomb in the Nigerian market and decide to duck into his cocoon in the belief that he should be let alone, citing democratic privacy, is more than deceit. It is akin to illusion if not delusion.

What is more? The case in question was seen as far from a mistake, which would have made it easier. Not a few saw the alarm by Kongi, as a deliberate propaganda, contrived to scare Nigerians and divert their attention from the main issue, which had to do with the rigged 2023 election. That the erudite statesman would still be defending this line of thinking even when there seems nothing at stake anymore as he did in the book about me is something that has left me aghast.

PETER OBI'S VICTORY AND SOYINKA'S ALTERNATIVE TRUTH

There is no doubt that Peter Obi, was Wole Soyinka's target in this entire saga. If there was any shred of such doubt, it was dispelled completely in that notorious South African outing where Kongi came out with his full chest to declare his stand. South Africa? Why the country of the Mandelas? That choice appears well made. There had been a buzz around the world, particularly in Africa and more particularly in South Africa, about the election.

In fact, many citizens of that country, had actually mocked Nigeria for the outcome and the crooked manner the Independent National Electoral Commission (INEC), handled the process. The buzzword was that Obi bested other competitors, including Bola Ahmed Tinubu, who was announced the winner and eventually sworn in as President.

So, the choice of the venue appeared quite deliberate. South Africa was a veritable ground to launch a pushback. And who was the best to do that than Soyinka, a Nobel Laureate and an international citizen, who not only commands a global audience attention, but whose words ought to command global credence as well.

So, as a guest speaker at the 2023 *Africa in the World* event, a festival that brings together the world's most innovative thinkers and top leaders to platform invigorating ideas for fresh changes and sustainable solutions for African people, he seized the moment to unleash his propaganda against Obi.

Themed: *The Lives of Soyinka – A Dialogue* he went to town: *This recent election – two things happened first of all. One party took over the labour movement, which is not my favourite movement, and then it became a regional party. Whereas it was a marvellous breach into the established two camps. Peter Obi achieved something remarkable there that he broke that mould. However, he did not win the election.*

I can say categorically that Peter Obi's party came third, not even second, and the leadership knew it, but they want to do what we call in Yoruba gbajue – that is force of lies. They were going to send some of the hardliners, proud young people into the street to demonstrate. I'm also ready to be among such demonstrators but only on the banner of truth, not on lies and deceit.

This party wanted the same thing (referring to 2011 post-election violence) to happen on the basis of a lie and we find this vice-presidential candidate on television boasting, insisting, threatening and trying to intimidate both the judiciary and the rest.

What kind of government will result from that kind of conduct? In addition, they did not know this but they were being used. Before the election, there were certain clandestine forces, including some ex-Generals who were already calling for an interim government before the elections began. Some of them were known figures, including a proprietor of a university, calling for an interim government before the election took place.

That was on Wednesday, September 23, 2023. Undeterred by the backlash and in an apparent boldface tactic, not only to push forward with his narrative, but browbeat his trolls, he dug deeper, this time in another statement on Saturday, September 26, entitled: *The Cape Town Re-Entry.*

Reiterating his earlier position, he said:

The mistake we all continue to make is our insistence on regarding the recent Nigerian elections as an adversarial thriller. The contrary is the truth. The ballot tally accurately reflected what happens when a political party splits itself in two, especially so critically close to an election. What promised to be a spectacular contest is transformed into a Feast of Voluntary Donation of the spoils of war.

"That, however, is not always the ultimate destination — the re-gifting may continue, prodded by a sudden surge of regret. There remains lurking in the background a far more potent beneficiary. In this case, we easily recall it as the unregistered but loudly canvassed IPP — the Interim Peoples Party, usually to be found in bed with the military. The notorious Datti interview — menacing, intimidating and unambiguous — sets the scene for such re-entry. Then history repeats itself over and over again, as currently manifested along the West African sub-region. The "call to arms" is made literal by those whose trade is precisely that of arms.

"Barring such abrupt "patriotic intervention", however, the last word belongs to the Supreme Court. Until that conclusive hour, wherever and whenever the subject turns to the Nigerian elections, my contribution can be taken for granted in advance: Peter

`Obi did not win the Nigerian 2023 elections.*

"Jointly with his erstwhile colleague of the PDP, Abubakar Atiku, they donated the outcome, even before the voting. Let politicians and their cohorts learn to take responsibility for the consequences of their choices within democratic options."

This was really where Soyinka touched the nerve of Nigerians at its most sensitive point. Not only Nigerians, but the world knew and still knows today that this was not the true picture of that event. The renowned sage, was only at his best with sophistry. Not even the most articulate string of words or highest display of erudition, as he laboured with in that outing or anywhere else, he tried to put up his well-celebrated literary skill, could convince anyone, including his audience at that forum that he was not being economical with the truth.

For sure, the world knew that Peter Gregory Obi won that election. The nearest point to the truth Soyinka was claiming, is that he lost the election the way Buhari lost his elections from 2003 up until the tables turned in the Nigerian electoral system in 2015. Before him, it was the same way Chief Obafemi Awolowo lost to Alhaji Shehu Shagari in 1979 and 1983. It is the Nigerian way – nay the African way – the undemocratic way of winning elections, where the first could easily become the last.

It is the model of electoral victories that have sustained the African variant of democracy in which the PDP, was so sure of retaining power that it served the world a notice through the late Vincent Ogbulafor, erstwhile National Chairman, who boasted that the party would rule Nigeria for 60 years, which at a point was even elevated to 100 years – the same model, which has made it as sure as death for political parties in power, to sweep all the local government election positions no matter how badly it performed or the credibility, worth, and acceptability of their candidates.

It is the model of elections that ensured that Obiang Teodoro of Equatorial Guinea, who came to power in 1979, has stuck there for a record 44 years, a record that makes him the longest in power in the entire world. It is the same type of elections that has kept Paul Biya of Cameroon in power since 6 November 1982 – 41 years despite ostensibly not being conscious of his immediate environment anymore and has to rely on aides to perform the most basic functions or even to move around.

There are more – Denis Sassou Nguesso of the Republic of Congo (39 years – 1979-1992 – 1997 till date), Uganda's Yoweri Museveni (37 years) since 1986, Isaias Afwerki of Eritrea (30 years since April 1993), Ismaïl Omar Guelleh, the current President of Djibouti who has been in power since 1999 after he was handpicked as successor to his uncle Hassan Gouled Aptidon who had ruled the country since independence in 1977. He was re-elected in 2005, 2011, and again in 2016.

It is the same model that is making Paul Kagame of Rwanda, who has remained for the past 23 years, the power and leeway to do so and is sure to make him 'win' the next elections should he desire to continue contesting. Today, that same electoral model is waiting to be exploited by Alassane Ouattara of Ivory Coast, who had to amend the constitution of the country to contest and 'win' a third term which he is still enjoying to date. Who knows what will happen by the time this current term runs out and he decides to run again? Not only would he succeed, but he would surely win.

Of course, Ali Bongo of Gabon would have bested the records of Omar Bongo, his father who died in office in June 2009 after more than 41 years, were it not for that inevitable end which came by the force of military power which removed him from office in 2023. It is the same with the late Gnassingbe Eyadema of Togo who ruled for 38 years from 1967 to his death in 2005 when his son took over.

Were he not ousted by his henchmen, who kept him in power, Zimbabwe's Robert Mugabe, who was forced out in November 2017 after 37 years at the helm, would have still been in office and so would Chad's Idriss Deby, who ruled for 31 years before his death on 19 April 2021. The intriguing aspect is that they not only professed democratic credentials but ensured that they remained in power through "elections" which they always "won," but "because the people loved them."

So, if it is on account of the wacky process, where the election is not based on the actual number of votes cast, but on the manipulations of the powers that be, who use state institutions to command victory – the type Fela Anikulapo-Kuti aptly described as democrazy – demonstration of craze – where election victory is working from the answer – then Soyinka is right.

But if the result of that election was about casting votes and counting them the way it is done in saner and safer climes and according to the prescription here in Nigeria, it is clear that the APC and Tinubu, the person announced as the winner, never got close to that outcome. On the other hand, anyone could stand atop the roof of Burj Khalifa in Dubai or Mount Everest to proclaim that Peter Obi won that election without fear of desecrating the lands or offending the heavens, because that is the real truth rather than the alternative truth the Kongi tried to sell to the world.

In making his narratives, Soyinka came out with some asser-tions which every passive observer could easily guess where it is coming from. These were claims that had all the elements of campaign darts thrown at Obi, especially from the APC camp. For instance, he claimed that Obi's campaign took a regional bent after taking over the LP.

Hear again:

"One party took over the labour movement which is not my fa-vourite movement and then it became a regional party. Whereas it was a marvellous breach into the established two camps. Peter Obi achieved something remarkable there that he broke that mould. However, he did not win the election." Imagine! How ingenious! How could anyone, who was in Nigeria and watched the massiveness and nationalistic nature of the Obidient Move-ment, ever reduce that phenomenon to a regional affair? How could anyone who was not emerging from a deep hole in the Amazon Forest or some caves in the ancient East Asian land of Mongolia, suggest that the LP, a party that was catapulted from its low-grade stature into a national platform, was a regional entity? That person must either be grossly ignorant or decidedly mischievous.

On the contrary, the LP was the only true national party at that time within the contest of Obi's membership and its association with the Obidients. In fact, it is the only political party whose membership could be found in every household in Nigeria be-cause of its clearly organic nature. Again, recall those eternal words of Godwin Obaseki:

"The future of our politics in this country is changing. I don't know

whether you are closely watching what is going on – the level of disenchantment with existing political parties – I'm sure in all our homes here, we have so many people now who call themselves Obidients. I don't know whether you have them in your house. Just ask them – all those children – just ask them in what party are you and they'll tell you it's Obidients.

"They don't want us. They're not talking about APC or PDP. They're looking for alternatives. And they're much, much more. You see all of them queuing for PVCs now. they're not looking in the direction of APC or PDP. They're looking for alternatives. If we don't make our party attractive, I don't know what will happen in the next elections."

Well, the answer the Edo governor sought, as to what would happen in the elections, was supplied early enough, as voting began on February 25 in the first set of the 2023 polls – sweeping votes for the LP. All over the country, from the East to the West, the North and the South, the evidence of the impact of the massive movement was clear. It was a tsunami. The Nigerian youths of the Gen Z era, had proved themselves as the owners of the votes. They even made a song and dance of their victory. Everywhere reverberated with pictorial and electronic evidence with videos of *Elupee 75, Elupee 87, Elupee 99!*

Alarm! Panic! Trepidation! *Our world is crumbling*, they must have shouted to themselves. Then they moved! *Government Magic*, that apt expression Fela Anikulapo depicted in his song, was rolled into motion. Green turned to red and white black. At the end of the day, they took care of the situation. They knew what to do. For the presidential election, they simply shut down the electronic system that stored the result – the INEC Result Viewing Portal (IReV), the mechanism devised by the Independent National Electoral Commission (INEC) to safeguard the integrity of the elections.

Once that was done, the rest was easy. Elections went back to what it was – a manipulative instrument in the hands of political vampires to take and retain power. Once elections returned to manual activities, the entire process crumbled. And so did the hope and confidence of Nigerians. Hours after, pictures of Nigerians in jubilation and celebrating the electoral victory, were replaced with those of pure melancholy, as real scenes of manual doctoring and manipulation of the results of the elections across the country, many of them with the active collaboration of security operatives and other institutional personnel loaned to ensure the integrity and security of the entire exercise, began hit the space. Now, this is what the Kongi is depicting in a different shape and form, when he told his audience and the world: *I can say categorically that Peter Obi's party came third, not even second, and the leadership knew it, but they want to do what we call in Yoruba gbajue – that is force of lies.* Really? Even the Nigerian literary icon himself, knows the truth about this claim. In fact, the world knows that if anyone was lying here, it was definitely not Peter Obi and his camp. The real culprit, was not far from the echoes coming from the microphone the sage used to pass his message.

Another assertion the Kongi made, was to the effect that the LP and PDP actually "donated" victory to the APC. In other words, if Obi and Atiku Abubakar, former Vice President and the PDP presidential candidate, had teamed up, they would have defeated Tinubu. Of course, this is another simplistic narrative of the APC to divert attention. The main issue of the 2023 presidential election was not about the figures, but INEC's deliberate manipulation and sexing up of figures to skew the result. Simplicita! It was a clear case of the true numbers and the fake ones.

Therefore, the truth is that even if the entire Chinese and Indian population was combined and made to come to Nigeria and vote for either Obi or Atiku, Tinubu would still have "won." Buhari was determined and sworn to that outcome. After all, did Atiku and Obi not team up as presidential and vice-presidential candidates in 2019 against Buhari, whose disastrous record as the worst President Nigeria has ever produced, is considered a national record? Never mind that Tinubu seems to have beat that record in just one year, today.

Did Buhari not "win?" Yes! The selfsame Buhari who, like Biya, was disgracing Nigeria on the international scenes because he appeared unaware of his environment – who at a press confer-ence in New York when asked a question on Nigeria's population, sprung out a written speech on climate change apparently pre-pared for him for a UN audience and began to read to reporters, to their utter amazement – beginning with "Your Excellencies" as if he was addressing heads of states, again, to the utter dismay of his audience – the same Buhari who was so debilitated that even the cool-headed Kaderia Ahmed, believed to be working for the APC, became so scandalised that she had to publicly chide Yemi Osinbajo, then Vice President, who accompanying him to the session, was constantly covering up for him. Remember – "he can speak for himself now" rebuke during her interview question where the former President would just shoot-off on a lone journey? Remember how the APC goons, including Rotimi Amaechi, former Governor of Rivers State, as Director of the Buhari campaign, were caught on camera shifting in their seats, with eyes popping out in exasperation, as their patron continued to embarrass the global audience, while veering off into a world of his own, in that interface with the interviewer?

Yet, he not only "won" the election thereafter, but even with a wider margin than he did in the 2015 edition that brought him in. It did not even matter that Nigerians, at that time, were already scraping the ground with their bare teeth, due to the myriads of economic and social malaise they had to face daily, including sleeping with two eyes open, due to the siege of insecurity.

So, the issue of donating votes to the APC did not arise. In fact, that Soyinka is toeing that line of argument, gave himself out completely. It underscored how much deep he was into the APC camp, because that narrative, was actually the popular line of the party and its supporters. They had used it and continued to use it to mitigate the case of the massive rigging that took place in that exercise. For emphasis, nothing would have made Obi win that election, even if the whole world population voted for him.

The outcome of that exercise, simply explained the principle of *Emilokan* (it's my turn) in full – that popular declaration Tinubu made in Abeokuta, the Ogun State capital on June 2, 2022, while addressing APC delegates.

It explained the absence of real campaigns - why he never did anything extra outside theatrics, to advance his pitch for the number one job- why public outings were sources of drama and comical reliefs rather than avenues to showcase his programmes or sell himself. It explained why the nuances of *Bala Blu, Bula-ba* at the Owerri town-hall meeting. It explained his raising his walking stick like a magician performing an act in Port Harcourt, while the national anthem was being sung – why in Kano he simply requested music because "I want to dance."

It explained why he merely sneered at those asking him to appear in debates with other opponents and why he dismissed such suggestions with a wave of the hand. It explained the true meaning of his oft-professed mantra that power is not given a la carte – but you have to grab it, snatch it, and run with it. He was simply too sure that he was going to win the election and that Buhari would transfer power to him willy-nilly. He never hid the reason for that confidence either.

Anyone in doubt should revisit that Abeokuta declaration where he gave some details of how he helped Buhari become President after failing on three previous occasions and the agreement that was reached that the Daura-born military General and former Head of State, would return the favour, by handing him back the baton at the end of the day.

What is more? Has anyone denied the statement made by Amaechi, who was rewarded with the princely Minister of Transportation by Buhari, that Mahmood Yakubu, the INEC Chairman, was appointed to his position by Tinubu? If true, what then is the implication for the supposed umpire? Could that not be the reason why the INEC boss broke the door with his bare feet in order to make Tinubu President, including announcing the result of the election in the wee-hours of March 1, 2023?

The most laughable of this tragi-comedy by the revered Soyinka, if not the most tragic, was the allegation of some form of insurrection or plot to truncate democracy he also made against Obi and his supporters, accusing the former Anambra governor of collaborating with some people to set the country on fire.

Listen to him:

"They were going to send some of the hardliners, proud young

people into the street to demonstrate. I'm also ready to be among such demonstrators but only on the banner of truth, not on lies and deceit. This party wanted the same thing (referring to 2011 post-election violence) to happen on the basis of a lie and we find this vice-presidential candidate on television boasting, insisting, threatening and trying to intimidate both the judiciary and the rest.

"What kind of government will result from that kind of conduct? In addition, they did not know this but they were being used. Before the election, there were certain clandestine forces, including some ex-Generals who were already calling for an interim government before the elections began. Some of them were known figures, including a proprietor of a university, calling for an interim government before the election took place."

That part actually got me. Did it sound familiar? Just like from the notebook of Abacha goons. Even the propaganda machinery of the despot, could not have done better or worse. Imagine linking Afe Babalola – the proprietor of a university – with such an odious scheme of plotting against his own country. Afe – that doyen of the legal profession, one of Nigeria's oldest members of the Inner Bar, known as Senior Advocate of Nigeria (SAN), now plotting undemocratic takeover of leadership in Nigeria. What audacity! What insult!

Perhaps more insulting was the apparent thought by the Nobel Laureate that he was going to mitigate the impact of his assertion by suggesting that the legal luminary was deceived into making that suggestion. How could Afe, a nonagenarian whose history sits on an award-winning platform of struggle and resilience at the initial stage of life and later a bouquet of experience in both law and hands-on knowledge of his environment, become so shallow as to be manipulated in the manner the Kongi was suggesting?

All the legal luminary, saw and warned about, came from fears that the current Constitution, if used to conduct another election, would plunge the country further into the morass of leadership crises it had suffered in years. The danger of an unrestructured Nigeria, especially with a constitution many considered a fraud to the extent of its use of the collective – *WE,* is not original to the erudite lawyer, but one even WS had also professed a zillion times.

How could the suggestion that Nigeria does not need to travel the same ruinous route of relying on its structure, be considered playing into the hands of anti-democratic forces plotting evil against the country? At the worst, could it simply not be considered one of the numerous interventions of Nigerians who do not love their country any less than the Kongi himself?

But with politics, especially of the Nigerian, nay African hue, what could be that surprising? Even the most reflective thoughts, practical suggestions, and credible solutions, no matter how benign and convincing, suffer the brickbats of suspicion and outright attacks once they are considered injurious to the goals of the entrenched interests.

How could a whole Kongi, lend himself to such an unwholesome scheme, travel that unpopular route, or be associated with such inglorious utterances? It was against this backdrop that brought about my intervention of September 19, 2023. In the piece titled: *Soyinka, Obi, Tinubu: When payment of mafia debt is inevitable*, published on *Whirlwindnews.com.ng,* I tried to explain to those who were stunned about the sudden metamorphosis of their revered icon that every man has a price. At the wedding in Cana, Jesus Christ had to bend backwards to perform the miracle of changing water into wine, because of His mother. All Mother Mary had to do was tell Her Son – *they have no wine* and left the rest to Him. Even though He protested at first and reminded Her that it was not time yet, the mother knew He would do it for Her sake. Thus, her further instruction to the people – *do whatever He tells you.*

If Jesus could go that length to please the Mother, who else could resist or become impenetrable to certain influences?

The import of my argument in that piece was that Soyinka and Tinubu were too closely-knit together by a long-standing relationship that both owed each other a strong debt, which the Kongi, was simply repaying at the time it mattered most. In doing so, I referred to Soyinka's own testimony. As Chairman of the fifth Bola Tinubu Colloquium held in Lagos on March 28, 2013, in honour of the *Jagaban Borgu*, the Nobel Laureate took a trip back, as he regaled the audience with some of the gripping details of their times during their NADECO days, as fugitives.

In that piece, I did not give details. Now I do. Hear from Kongi himself:

As you know he (Tinubu) was a fugitive offender like many of us here. Former governor of Lagos State and also a businessman. Some of us in the anti-Abacha movement won't have survived if not for him.

During our period of exile resistance, we looked for all kinds of means to raise funds including trying to print redeemable bonds. I think we did print redeemable bonds. We were so confident of victory and we said let's print bonds and sell those bonds. We designed those bonds... The symbol that we were supposed to use as at that time which was to be symbolic of growth, because it was a shrub, apparently that shrub looked like marijuana. We didn't know this until someone pointed it out.

But finally, Bola Tinubu said what do we have to do? We have to find funds. I said what can you do; you are the businessman and he (Bola) said I heard there's a rice line between Taiwan and other places. I think I can get a contract to sell rice between Taiwan and Africa. I said go ahead and sell rice.

He said they would require a letter of recommendation and Bola said I have to write one, but I replied him I don't know anything about rice and Bola told me that I should write that we are trading in rice and give the letter to me and I will give the government of Taiwan and they would supply the rice to me and I sell the rice and use the money for revolution.

So when I came back from exile, my house had been made inhabitable, I took a place in Lagos while my house was being fixed. I found out the work was slow while I was in Lagos. So I got this reasonably cheap house. We moved in there. It was an unfinished house. But suddenly a vehicle rode up and I thought the vehicle contained bags of rice from Taiwan but it was pots and pans. What more do you require if you are moving to an unfinished building? You need to cook. His wife, Remi Tinubu, had thought that I would need those items for me and my wife to survive before our house is repaired in Ogun State.

You see! I did not have water in my mouth when I made that connection. You heard the Kongi himself say it that some of them could not have survived the Abacha onslaught without Tinubu finding a way to raise funds to cater for the financial crisis within that struggle. Personally, even though I feel the Kongi, was actually exaggerating and might be speaking figuratively, because it is impossible for him to ever go hungry on this planet earth for any reason, given his status, I believe that his anecdote was still quite germane in many contexts.

In his reply through *Baiting Igbophobia: The Sunny Igboanugo Thesis*, Kongi reminded me that he was the one who wrote the letter of recommendation for the Taiwan rice and not Tinubu as I wrote in my piece and that it was during the struggle and not after. I stand corrected. But that mix-up does not in any way detract from the facts of the matter or destroy the message therein. The emphasis was that the Nobel Laureate, intent on paying a debt, was only helping an old friend defeat the avalanche of discontent by throwing his national and international weight into the arena. It had nothing to do with a Yusuf Datti Baba-Ahmed preparing for war, Peter Obi inciting Nigerian youths to violence, or Obidients plotting insurrection.

Indeed, the first call Obi made after INEC pronounced Tinubu winner of the election in the wee hours of March 1, 2023, was for calm, which immediately calmed nerves and put paid to any plan of demonstration or street protests. He had expressed his belief that the courts would overturn the results because he believed the evidences were as visible as a sore thumb.

PART TWO

The 2023 presidential election, would ordinarily have been no different from the previous exercises in Nigeria. It had the same trappings – same environment, same players. Then Obi happened. He was a precious political find, like a prized gem buried in the ground, which was discovered and placed on a national pedestal, from where his glittering light illuminated across the nation and beyond.

His emergence on the larger Nigerian political scene was quite sudden, instant, and dramatic. Arguably his sterling rendition in Anambra State as a two-term governor, was probably known by only the indigenes of the state. Some few across the country, who did, could actually be from the headlines that had to do with his several court victories. He had in 2006 dethroned Chris Ngige, the Anambra governor at the centre of the kidnapping saga in the state in 2003. Remember the hullabaloo about a sitting governor spirited away from his desk on July 10, 2003 by security agents. He was eventually ousted by Obi in 2006, a historic event that made headlines. Recall also that it was the same Obi that sacked Andy Uba as governor of the same Anambra on January 14, 2007, in the landmark *Tenure Interpretation* case that changed the structure of elections in Nigeria.

Yes! Three years of a dreary court process after the 2003 governorship election in Anambra State, Obi, who contested on the platform of the All Progressives Grand Alliance (APGA), was able to oust Ngige, the candidate of the PDP, who was initially declared winner. But that was not all. Having spent just barely one year in office, Ubah was sworn in as the governor in 2007, on the ground of that year's governorship election. Obi returned to the courts, this time the Supreme Court for the now famous tenure interpretation. The apex court agreeing with him that he ought to enjoy his full four-year tenure as prescribed by the constitution, sacked Ubah and asked him to return to office.

This streak of court victories, including prevailing over members of the Anambra State House of Assembly, which subsequently impeached him and returning to power via court pronouncements, were not enough to give him the national leverage he enjoys today. Not even the fact that he was lapped up when his second tenure ended in 2014 by then President Goodluck Jonathan, as one of his economic advisers, gave him that influence. What did, was that outing on October 1, 2016, when he mounted the rostrum as one of the guest speakers at *The Platform*, a yearly national speaking event organised by Poju Oyemade, Senior Pastor and founder of The Covenant Nation (TCN). Speaking on the topic – *Cutting the Cost of Governance*, Obi not only used personal anecdotes of his days in Government House Agu Awka in Anambra State to rouse his audience, especially the Nigerian youths, but got himself etched permanently in their hearts. That was the day he sold himself to the people.

Having broken into national consciousness by the stellar performance he pulled off at that event, where his speech, was punctuated by intermittent standing ovations never witnessed in the same hall where the event had held for the past 18 years, it became the turning point into his political life. His voice had echoed not only around the hall but in the hearts of virtually every youth in Nigeria, to whom he left an enduring message – *take back your country.*

Hear how Oyemade captured Obi's outing:

When I invited former Anambra State Governor Peter Obi to speak at the 2016 edition of 'Platform Nigeria' I had not met him before. In fact, I only met him in person for the first time two hours before his speech on October 1. But his intervention on the waste that defines governance in our country today has touched a very deep nerve with many Nigerians, including me. Indeed, I strongly believe that the political elite will be making a big mistake if they think the landscape will remain the same after such a revealing presentation.

It did not. Indeed, like Patrick Henry's *Give Me Liberty or Give Me Death* speech, delivered at the Second Virginia Convention on March 23, 1775, rousing the hearts of citizens towards liberating America from the authorities of Britain, Obi's was his own battle-cry for Nigerian liberation. Since then, the Nigerian youths, have not only owned the war but have practically taken ownership of Obi as the commander to lead the battles in the field.

Naturally, Obi would have begun his quest immediately after that outing, but for the dynamics of Nigerian politics. The North still had one more term left given the Nigerian North-South political arrangement and throwing his hat into the ring would amount to a lack of political wisdom. It was no surprise that he became the first choice when Atiku was searching for a running mate for the 2019 election. He had to be. His immense popularity was all the former Vice President needed to coast high.

But again, democracy, *a la* Africa, happened with the first becoming the last once more. Instead of benefitting from the blinding defeat they both delivered to Buhari on February 23 through the thumbs of Nigerians, who wanted nothing more to do with that disastrous era in their country and could not wait to see its back, this was not to be, as the political buccaneers went to work once again using their usual tools – government institutions. Naturally, the country lost again.

But Obi remained resolute. Instead of losing energy or focus, he became the true conscience of the country. Most times he became the lone voice challenging the Buhari misgovernance at every turn. His voice continued to reverberate across the country and beyond about the wasteful spending in government and its sheer over-bloated size.

He was the lone voice that continued to warn both the government and Nigerians about the impending disaster as part of the consequences from Buhari's penchant for indiscriminate borrowings to satisfy bogus lifestyles of privileged people in government.

Obi, cried his voice hoarse about the impact of borrowing to eat instead, of borrowing to produce. He not only provided evidence of how it was done in other countries that succeeded, but figures on how they did it. He counselled, he remonstrated, he warned but, he was ignored.

Sadly, instead of taking counsel, Buhari and his men pilloried, taunted and scoffed at him. But Nigerians listened. They knew he was not only speaking the truth but he was speaking for them and their children. Not only did they listen to him, they followed him especially when they dug deep and discovered that he lived what he preached. They discovered that everything he told them was true, including his sterling records in Anambra State.

Which other governor in Nigeria would leave a whopping N75 billion for his successor instead of pocketing it and facing the law with a fraction of it? Obi not only told them how he did it but asked them to go and verify?

In that *PLATFORM* outing, he told his audience how he saved the money – stopping the daily killing of cows in government house to cook for the first family – how he ended the endless party-ing and quaffing of expensive wines in government house – even how he would personally supervise the purchase of petrol at filling stations – simple everyday activities witnessed elsewhere that made governments not only accountable but their officials work for the people in other climes.

Obi was not just talking history; he was actually practical. He nei-ther lied nor claimed glory for what he did not do for political advantage. He claimed only those things he achieved and told them to verify.

For example, in 2021 there was a news flash that went viral on social media and even the traditional platforms that Peter Obi had donated a whopping N1 billion to the Nigerian effort towards curbing the menace of COVID-19, the deadly pandemic that was ravaging the world at that time.

Whoever initiated that story might have done so with some nega-tive intentions, either to catch cruise, to chase clout or simply to rope him into a particular corner. On the other hand, the person could also have had the positive intention of promoting him, per-haps believing that linking him with such a huge donation was likely to paint him in good light as a philanthropist in the mould of the late Moshood Kashimawo Olawale (MKO) Abiola, whose proclivity to public-spiritedness and philanthropy was believed to have opened so many doors for him during his quest to become President of Nigeria, which he would have been had the military that prosecuted the 1993 presidential election not annulled it in the infamous June 12 saga.

So, give or take, it could either have been for the reasons above or anything else. However, what appeared strange at that time and now was that the former governor instantly debunked the story. Unlike many other politicians who would have hugged the story, true or false, for the obvious advantage of projecting them as first well-to-do as to give out such an amount freely for public purpose or humanitarians with the heart of gold, he flatly denied doing so.

What is more? He was named alongside Aliko Dangote, Africa's Richest Man, said to have donated the same amount for the same purpose. Which politician would not seize such a moment to shine? But not Obi. Rather, in a statement by Valentine Obi-enyem, his spokesman, he wished those who were making the contribution then under what was later dubbed Ca-COVID well.

But do you know what? That same week, he established his own intervention programme. From his personal finances, he super-vised the procurement of the essentials for the same COVID-19 initiatives and their distribution to target groups and practically witnessed all the processes from point A to point Z.

What was the result of that? The Ca-COVID initiative, which net-ted over N21 billion at the last count with individuals, banks, and groups making huge donations as with other Nigerian public in-stitutions, became mired in controversy with a lot of questions hanging on its head because of the opaque nature of the man-agement of the huge funds.

In the end, what came out of the loud talks of erecting infrastruc-ture, procurement of machinery and drugs, and the concomitant programmes of testing, isolation and treatment centres and other tall projects simply evaporated. Yet that of Obi became a reference point in terms of efficiency and effectiveness.

While nobody actually came out to testify to benefitting from the former, pictures and videos of beneficiaries from Obi's little efforts were all over the space.

From the available picture, he must have spent a lot, far beyond the N1 billion he was said to have donated. But even though that huge financial commitment was a mere fraction of the Ca-COVID effort, the difference was clear in terms of the result.

The reason for this outcome ought to be clear even to an imbecile. It simply adumbrates the fact in the traditional saying that a goat fed by the public usually dies of hunger because nobody actually takes responsibility.

This is exactly the sickness with Nigeria. The truth is that the running of Nigeria must be taken as a personal business. Those leading the country must have the capacity and the presence of mind to go through the gamut of its daily activities with a fine-comb. In other words, Nigeria must not only be run by a leadership with the right sentiments and national emotions but one that is not only present but involved always.

This was just one example. Sample another instance. In May 2018, a melodrama took place in Ukana, a nondescript community in the Nsukka area of Enugu State. It was at the burial of Lady Bibiana Adani, an elder sister to the former governor, who was married to the community. Being a former governor, the people had expected a big event, a lavish ceremony of eating and drinking. After all, their in-law was a big man a la Nigeria. Who would have blamed them? Elsewhere so many cows would have lost their heads and all roads would have led to the village. It would have been an occasion to see the big men of the country with their long convoys of exotic cars, exotic lifestyles and other accoutrements of opulence, pomp and ceremonies.

But what did they see? They did not even recognise their in-law when he slipped in like every ordinary folk and when they finally did, they were disappointed that there were no crisp notes to be flung in the air, neither did they get plenty of rice, meat and other delicacies to be eaten and taken away in the bags some of them were armed with.

Naturally, they cursed their luck. Where were the foods and drinks? Where were the mobile phones and other exotic souvenirs that were the lot of other communities that were lucky to produce such a big man? What stinginess! What ill-luck!

But they did not understand that Obi was not their usual customer. Hear his side:

Sometimes I shudder at what people do for the dead as if they are a marketing commodity. All the dead need from the living is a decent burial after they must have taken care of him or her while living. As a Catholic, what I owe her now are prayers and booking of masses for the happy repose of her soul and not an opportunity to display wealth that should rather be used to add value to humanity. We're unnecessarily spending money in burials and other celebrations. What we usually spend in a week on burials or other social events can rehabilitate over a hundred schools and at least can be used to build a factory.

But did the former governor leave the people empty-handed? Never! Rather he gave them something different, something no other person would have contemplated but more enduring that would continue to affect their lives decades even more than when all the people who attended that ceremony and were angry that they did not eat rice and meat must have themselves disappeared from the surface of the earth.

Hear him:

I personally shunned advertisements and other gifts from people in support of the burial of my sister. Rather I asked anybody that wanted to buy anything for me to give me the cash. My plan is to use the money collected to rehabilitate a school as well as build a brand-new Health Centre in honour of late Bibiana at Adani Ukana where she was married. I think she will be happier that her death has brought succour to the people rather than in the number of cows killed for her which may end up causing health issues to some people.

Even from the angle of creating unnecessary burden to ourselves, have you asked yourself the stress involved in countless calls and emails to people for condolence messages that would be published in a brochure? I mean all these things are unnecessary burdens?

Did this sound familiar with politicians? How many politicians had spoken or would ever speak in this manner?

The foregoing events were just two of the numerous practical examples Obi used to demonstrate that he was of a different hue and that he was in politics for other reasons and not the primordial ends and that his getting a chance to take charge of the levers of power at the national level would present a completely new paradigm in the socio-political firmaments of the country. Nigerians listened. Nigerians bought his story. Nigerians acted.

LIKE ABIOLA, LIKE OBI

In contemporary Nigerian history, the only personality or politician, so to speak, that evoked similar sentiments to Peter Obi is probably the late Moshood Kashimawo Olawale (MKO) Abiola. But there was a huge difference. Despite creating a similar momentum, the two presented different contrasting personas. The reason Abiola was known all over Nigeria, Africa, and the world sharply contrasted with that of Obi.

Abiola was flamboyance personified – a man of influence and character. He was the business mogul, owner of many companies and establishments including the influential *Concord Newspapers*, a status that catapulted him to the position where he rubbed shoulders with world leaders and even reputed to have installed presidents in Africa and beyond. He was a godfather and a kingmaker. Husband to many wives and father of many children. Whoever needed money went to him. His immense wealth reflected in his ownership of Abiola Babes Football Club. He was the Pillar of Sports in Africa and patron of many organisations and bodies. He was not only a great philanthropist but *The Money Man*.

On the contrary, Obi presents a different picture. Despite being a man of means himself, once reputed in some quarters to be among the 8000 richest men in the world, he maintains a prudent, measured, moderate and even austere mien. Unlike

Abiola, whose philanthropic gestures had no restraint as he gave to virtually everyone that came in contact with him no matter the status, Obi though also a philanthropist in his own way structures all his actions concerning money. Obi's donations were and are still tailored to schools and hospitals and never to ordinary events. He did not give freely. He did not give to please; he gave for specific purpose – fit for purpose donations.

So, while it is likely that young couples planning their weddings could get mouth-watering donations from Abiola or town unions celebrating end-of-the-year activities would likely smile home after writing Abiola for assistance, Obi would most likely not donate to such events. To Abiola, money could be for pure pleasure while for Obi it must be applied to advance a cause.

This sharp difference became evident in how each of them emerged as candidates for their individual political parties. Abiola was said to have bought his ticket by matching the likes of Shehu Musa Yar'Adua money for money at the Social Democratic Party (SDP) convention in Jos, Plateau State in 1993. He was said to have given double of what his opponents spent to the delegates who decided at the primaries.

On his part, Obi, in his surprise letter notifying the National Chairman of his resignation on May 20, 2022 from the PDP, was initially silent on his reason. He later told Nigerians that he ditched the former ruling party and ended his presidential ambition on its platform, despite the better prospect due to the massive influence of money. The former governor was particularly scandalised by the manner the process was dollarised, saying it was not healthy for his spirit as a Nigerian.

Here was how he explained his decision: His exact words:

I'm not desperate to be president; I'm desperate to see Nigeria work, especially for the youth. I've moved to a party where I think the system will allow me to contribute. I'll rather lose doing the right thing than win doing the wrong thing. My politics has been consistent in character and integrity throughout the time I started. You can go and check.

This is not the first time I left PDP. In 2002, when I started this politics, I was a member of PDP. I went to one meeting and I want to contribute and some people said no, you cannot contribute. I quietly left and went to APGA. I went to APGA, campaigned and won an election and somebody else was declared. I didn't quarrel and I went to court. I became the first Nigerian to ever stay in court for three years and I didn't quarrel until I was declared winner.

A few days after this remarkable statement, Obi joined the Labour Party (LP), then one of the low-grade political platforms in Nigeria that barely came into reckoning except for some marginal past performances that only managed to keep it from being deregistered. It was this strategic move that truly announced the former governor on the podium of national politics in the most peculiar way.

Pat Utomi, one of Nigeria's most prolific and erudite scholars of international repute who was on the verge of picking the party's ticket as the presidential candidate for the coming election, stepped down alongside two other contenders. That was how the ticket was handed down to Obi without sweat at the LP convention that took place in Asaba on May 30, 2022.

In an interview with Vanguard, published on June 3, 2022, the accomplished scholar and banker, who in his own rights could be listed as one of the members in the exclusive club of few Nigerians usually addressed as the Conscience of the Nation, as he gave reasons for dumping his own ambition in favour of Obi explained:

We have to look at the bigger picture. Our country is in a desperate situation. Nigeria is on the verge of collapse. From the point of view of finance, Nigeria is purely bankrupt. States are not paying salaries. Ostensibly we have spent over 400 billion on so-called subsidies this year and very few people are willing to lend to Nigeria.

The corruption in the system is frightening that every part of that so-called subsidy is corruption. We don't have the political courage to do what should be done so we are rotten in that territory. And as a country we are economically crippled.

When we come to security, more people are killed in Nigeria every day than anywhere in the world. So, Nigeria is in a rolling civil war even though it pretends that it's not in a war. In terms of moral order, Nigeria has collapsed. The Academic Staff Union of Universities (ASUU) has been on strike for months and students are out of the universities. All the money these lecturers are asking for to fix the system is a small fraction of what one man stole.

If you treat issues as 'business as usual' and make party conventions where they exchange dollars, you are essentially inviting a bloody revolution. In other words, the political class is inviting a bloody revolution. They are not smart at all. They can't even see that if the things continued like this that they would be slaughtered in the streets of Nigeria.

So, seeing all these problems and then thinking about me or my ego is madness. My entire life in politics has never been about me, it has always been about how to better the common good of all. I don't know about others but I am probably the only one who has put everything into politics and probably lost so much but I don't care because history is the judge that matters. We did everything to bring the All Progressives Congress (APC) to power but the night after the election, they considered us dangerous because we can ask questions. That was the last day I heard from President Muhammadu Buhari's Administration. No government has ever excluded me from even listening to my ideas in Nigeria's history more than Buhari's government. None!

It shows how afraid they are of the truth. See what they have done to Nigeria. We fought for an anti-corruption government but ended up with the most corrupt government in Nigeria's history. So, when you have that level of crisis, you need to make desperate choices. The first choice before us is how to liberate Nigeria from Nigerian politicians. The second is how to save Nigerians from the dollarisation of their politics. These are what we need to stop.

In stopping this you have to accept the idea of a man who said 'sorry I am not going to use Dollars to go to party primaries.' So, my recognising Peter Obi was because of the statement he made. And that is a worthy statement to make. I have been in this struggle for nearly 50 years. Next year it will be 50 years since I have been organising students to topple the student union.

I have struggled for 50 years to make Nigeria a better country and I am not complaining that I lost continually but I am more worried that despite my efforts Nigeria is about to go under. So, what is bigger than one more effort if that would help turn Nigeria around?

Peter is younger than I and he would have more energy to do more of these things than me. Secondly Peter respects my opinion. He comes to me, calls on me even when he was the governor of Anambra State. I thank God I can pay my bills, have a roof over my head which is the most important thing about life.

Nigerian politicians are yet to discover the beauty of a simple life. Politicians are not supposed to be rich men. They are supposed to be people who humbly give up themselves to advance the common good. Ghanaian highlife musician Ben Brako made this immortal statement: 'If you see a country where their politicians are richer than their businessmen, you see a country which is about to collapse.'

Nigeria is a classic example of a country where their politicians are richer than their businessmen. Businessmen have to go cap-in-hand to the politicians so that their businesses can continue to exist. That is a country that wants to collapse and we want to pull out our country from that brink.

For me, if Nigeria is to have any hope of progress, the starting point is to stop the APC and Peoples Democratic Party (PDP) from being relevant in Nigerians' lives. So, I felt we should pull energy to achieve the same goal rather than forcing it. I have invested over three years of my life trying to proclaim the Labour Party and make it a platform for workers on how Nigeria is governed. Peter Obi has been able to catch the attention of young people.

So, I choose to take on the position of the leader of the party. Like I said in Asaba, I chose to become the Group Managing Director and Peter is the Managing Director (MD) because he is younger than me, he has more energy and in my role as GMD my job is to build the big tent to get the other parties to join us so we can redeem our country through that.

For me, I don't call APC and PDP two parties. I refer to them as one party. They are two wings of one party. We have a single-party state structure in Nigeria. Some of their members can be in APC in the morning, PDP in the afternoon and back to the APC in the evening. The movement is very fluid.

The single-party structure has managed Nigeria to the grave. Look at power. In 22 years, we are worse now than we were in 1999. In Cote d'Ivoire, Alassane Quattara has fixed the problem, why were these people unable to do something in 22 years? It is because there is a fundamental character flaw in the DNA of the PDP and APC.

God said in the scripture 'I set before you life and death, choose life that you may live.' It is clear that what these two parties have offered us is death. What is being said to Nigerians is to choose life that you may live. That is a fundamental philosophical issue. That is the reason that I pursued the labour movement. The Labour movement has a big structure covering workers across the country in the Nigeria Labour Congress (NLC); Trade Union Congress (TUC) etc. With the Labour Party fully in, we have a national structure.

Secondly, we have an initiative called the 40 million ballots initiative. The idea of the initiative is to invite 40 million new voters. If we succeed in registering 20 to 30 million new voters and these people (riggers) manage to take money from the government treasury to give them, if there are 30 million new voters, they won't find enough money to give these new voters.

Now if anyone is looking for the reason for the Obi explosion-23, read carefully these profound words of Utomi. They provide every answer to the Peter Obi phenomenon – the essence – the raison d'être. In the first place, that Obi refused to play the money politics was not a function of his deep pocket or lack of it, but rather a matter of principle.

Indeed, if he had decided to go that route, there were multiple Nigerian godfathers who would have been willing to sponsor him with enough funding capable of giving him a fair chance in the money contest. His popularity would have earned him that support from the moneybags. All he needed was to trade in his credibility, which typical of Nigerian politics he could even repudiate or deny on assuming power.

Again, on his own, given his individual status as a wealthy man with vast interest in big businesses such as banking, manufacturing and trading, he could even muster enough money himself that would put him in good stead to make a go at the PDP ticket such that even if he does not get it, he could be considered one of the godfathers of the party – a status which would position him at the sharing table of the Nigerian commonwealth.

So, turning his back on money politics was out of choice rather than capacity or incapability. His declaration to always do the right thing regardless of the odds was not only completely new but sweet music to the ears of Nigerians. The resonating message was not lost. Instead, its echo reverberated in the hearts of the people who took it further, advancing it as their own.

"We're Obidients, we no de give shishi!" This soon became the catchphrase on the lips of virtually every Nigerian youth. It had a grander effect. For the first time, Nigerian youths did not expect anything from Nigerian politicians. This mantra was not demonstrated in words only but in deeds. The youths, through what

later became the Obident Movement, practically took ownership of the Obi ambition and the process of achieving it. For there, they saw the new Nigeria in which their future was to be assured.

So, while Abiola adopted a top-to-bottom approach in 1993, where he unleashed his immense financial capacity to buy up the political space up to the June 12 presidential election and even beyond, Obi's model presented completely different and contrasting features.

In 1993, the business magnate, outside funding the SDP machinery, which had its offices nationwide through which it did its own things, also provided for coordinators and other interest groups down to the wards across the country, all of which he funded directly from his personal pocket. Outside the headquarters of the *Hope '93* campaigns and other offices across the country, which on their own were bee-hives, Abiola's personal home in Ikeja, Lagos, presented its own picture of a marketplace with many of the traders, most of them mere opportunists in search of what seemed the bottomless pit of the billionaire's wealth, milling around and practically stabbing each other in the back to inch closer to him.

But for Obi, it was a different ballgame. Most of the members of the Obident Movement catered for their own events. On their own, they created clusters. In the streets, the wards, through the states, and up to the national level, individuals sponsored meetings, farmed out functions, and funded operations on their own. They printed memorabilia, created unique messages, and took over social media, their natural habitat as youths.

Obidients hired buses to campaign venues, provided campaign materials, shared food and water donated by members, and printed banners, flyers, posters, and other informational materials. Many content creators made Obi the centre of their individual skits and countered anti-campaign forces.

Accentuated by Obi's political sagacity and robust engagements, coupled with unusual energy, grit of character, and uncommon courage, which made him traverse even the most dreaded parts of the country, including parts of Boko Haram-infested areas of Borno State, a political behemoth of iconic dimension was created both in Nigeria and beyond. It was an organic movement that had its roots and branches spreading in the remotest parts of the world.

In the US, UK, Canada, Sweden, and virtually all parts of the world, Obidient Movement cells were created to raise funding for the campaign efforts. In fact, but for the legal implication which puts a ceiling on diaspora funding, Nigerians living in these countries had actually elected to fund the entire campaign. It was the first time such an organic movement was ever created in recent political history of Nigeria.

A more intriguing aspect of the story is that this massive support had no barriers or boundaries. It came from Nigerians of all ethnic groups, religious persuasions, and all classes and ages. The common denominator was that these people who had seen things work in these countries knew that it was no rocket science and could be replicated back home in their own country.

They were able to connect with Obi as his message resonated among them. Actually, many of them, particularly those who were secure enough, even returned home to participate in the Obi project. Apart from coming home to mobilise people, many registered and either stayed home throughout the process to cast their votes, while others returned to base after registration only to return home to vote for Obi. Many who could not were on constant telephone calls with their folks back home. Others used social media to pass their message. It was clear that they wanted to put their money where their mouth was. For that, they neither kept quiet nor prevaricated.

Outside these prevailing sentiments, other factors made Obi's project quite attractive. For many others outside the youth and diaspora groups, especially the older generations, it was all about the primordial sentiments that underscored the nation's political and leadership structure. This was the time to promote the time-tested principle of equity, justice, and fair play.

Historically, the Igbo in Nigeria are the third leg of the Nigerian tripod and are seen as such by many. But they have not only continuously held the wrong end of the stick but have been hard done by in many ways, including politically, where for many decades they had been denied a place at the lunch table. Obi's presidency would have solved and ended all these prevailing ethnic sentiments.

This was the sentiment behind the argument of the regional bodies such as the Afenifere, the pan-Yoruba socio-cultural organisation, the Pan-Niger Delta Development Forum (PANDEF), and Middle Belt Forum (MBF). Of course, Ohanaeze Ndigbo was like the household of the agitation, having been the channel through which the campaign against the marginalisation of the Igbo was spread.

For the leadership of the groups, Ayo Adebanjo of the Afenifere, Edwin Clark of the PANDEF, and Britus Pogo for MBF were not only relentless in their campaigns but forceful in their arguments on why it must be Obi – particularly the part that he was the balm that would heal the festering wound the nation had been carrying about since the crisis that began in 1966 through the civil war to the present-day Nigeria, permanently.

Of them all, Adebanjo was the most frontal, audacious, and fiercely virulent. For him, the South East producing the next President would fully echo all the Yoruba nation stood for – equity, justice, and fair play, and the contrary would be completely antithetical as it would reflect greed, a vice the people were never identified with. How could the Yoruba nation, after Obasanjo took the first slot and ran his full course from 1999 to 2007 and Yemi Osinbajo, another Yoruba, became the Vice President between 2015 and 2023, be angling to produce the President again through Tinubu when the Igbo had not produced either since 1999?

This was the crux of the argument he presented as the Afenifere position at every turn. *The Yoruba will not take its turn and take the turn of another person just because he has the advantage or power to do so,* he continued to admonish in the most strident manner. He called meetings, granted interviews, and held press conferences to explain this position. For those who challenged the quality of his Yoruba, he challenged them to present a contrary argument and prove they were more Yoruba than him.

Challenged about the endorsement of Obi, here is what he told Arise News:

Why are we supporting Obi? The constitutional, logical, and equitable reasons for it, I have stated. Those are the issues they should address. They should tell us that the rotation system which showed that Yoruba have had their slot and automatically disqualifies Tinubu now is false.

None of them can claim to love the Yoruba people more than me, Ayo Adebanjo; no Yoruba man living. I am challenging them to come out if there is any organisation in existence that surpasses Afenifere in protecting Yoruba interest.

This is not a Yoruba matter; it's not a contest between Yoruba and Igbo. It is about who are the best champions of the people. This is an equitable thing for the unity of the country. That is what we should address. We should first decide whether we should have a second chance when one of us has not had a chance.

Those are facts of the issue. We are not only opposed to the issue of Tinubu; we are also opposed to Atiku. How can a Fulani man rule for eight years and another Fulani man is going back there? Those are the issues. Let us base this election on issues, not on sentiments.

And if you read that statement where I first announced our support for the South East, I didn't even know who was going to be the candidate then; it was principle and certain ideals. It is that ideal they should challenge.

They should not bring in any price line or sentimental attachment. I won't accuse them of any other ulterior motive; that's their affair, but that is our own case; it is the case that they should address; address the message, forget the messenger.

Accompanying Obi on his campaign to Ibadan, capital of the Yorubaland, the nonagenarian again told the Yoruba nation at the Adamasingba Stadium:

Don't let tribal sentiments influence your vote in the 2023 presidential election.

We cannot continue to demand that the Igbo people remain in Nigeria while we at the same time continue to brutally marginalise and exclude them from the power dynamics. Peter Obi is the person of Igbo extraction that Afenifere has decided to support and back. He is the man we trust to restructure the country back to federalism on the assumption of office.

We will not compromise this principle of justice, equity, and inclusiveness because one of our own, Asiwaju Bola Tinubu, is a frontline candidate. It is on this same principle we condemn the People's Democratic Party for sponsoring Atiku Abubakar, a Northern Fulani Muslim, to succeed General Muhammadu Buhari, another Fulani Muslim.

At a press conference two days after the Ibadan outing, Adebanjo again told reporters in Lagos:

The current President is a Fulani from the Northwest, and by virtue of the zoning arrangement that has governed Nigeria since 1999, power is supposed to return to the south imminently.

The southwest, as I have pointed out, has produced a president and currently sits as VP; the South-South has spent a total of six years in the Presidency, but the Igbo people of the South-East have never tasted presidency in Nigeria, and now that the power is due back in the South, equity demands that it be ceded to the Igbo.

For Clark, he had started shouting about the South East producing the next President early enough. Almost immediately after Buhari's second term began in May 2019, he told all ears that cared to listen that the next President must not only come from the South but the South East. This much was stressed in an interview published in Vanguard of October 6, 2019, where he not only drummed his message home but even warned against Tinubu, another Yoruba man's entrance in the race.

Hear him:

When Lord Lugard amalgamated us, he did not say northerners are superior to southerners. They had the presidency several times throughout the military era. Today, another northerner is running for eight years. The South-West have had their turn and the South-South had their turn through President Jonathan. It is only the South-East that has not had it. It is the turn of the Igbo to have it. Where in Nigeria don't you have competent people? Where in Nigeria don't you have intelligent people? Every region in Nigeria has qualified people to run government and be President of Nigeria. That is why people like Alhaji Balarabe Musa and Senator Shehu Sani are talking of giving peace a chance. Let zoning between the South and the North continue. That is the only honest thing to do in this country.

Reminded that Tinubu was warming up and was likely to get it based on his relationship with Buhari, he said:

What does Tinubu have to offer that the people of the South-East cannot offer? What is the justification for them to become the President of Nigeria? Is it because they belong to the APC? They should not be thinking of how to divide Nigeria. We must all unite and have respect for ourselves. The South-West should allow other people to have a taste of power. There is no way the South-West would be better than the South-East on the 2023 presidency.

Pogu was no less emphatic in trading in and stating the position of the MBF. In an interview with Arise News weeks before the election, he narrated how the group was instrumental to Obi exiting the PDP because they felt that his ambition was threatened there to underscore how much they were interested in the South East not only producing the next President but how much his candidature appealed to his group.

Hear him:

It is quite clear. We are supporting his candidacy. We actually supported his emergence because when we said yes to be fair, somebody from the South East should come up, we contacted our brothers from the South East, the Ohanaeze Ndigbo and the South East leaders. So many processes went through, and Peter Obi had to leave the PDP and moved to Labour Party. Irrespective of which party, ours is a struggle for better Nigeria, and the better Nigeria we feel can be guaranteed by his candidature and with him being elected as the President of the country.

So, we are supporting Peter to be the candidate of the Labour Party to be President of Nigeria because we believe that all per-mutations that he is the person with Datti Baba-Ahmed by his side as the Vice to help Nigeria out of what it is facing now. They are both young, intelligent, and they have track record and that compared to the others they stand shoulder-high above the oth-ers.

Ours is not about structure and all that. People are the structure. You can't just wish the people away, whether it is the youths, the women and whatever, because they are Nigerians. As long as votes will count, I can assure you, you will be amazed at the kind of votes that will be cast for them. The Middle Belt, particularly through the guidance of the Middle Belt Forum, will vote for Pe-ter Obi massively.

But among the greatest endorsements was to come from former

President Olusegun Obasanjo! Two major implications here! Apart from his immense influence as Nigeria's longest leader, dead or alive – three years as Military Head of State and eight years as civilian President – a profile through which he built a humongous authority not only in Nigeria, Africa, and even across the globe, he is a Yoruba man. In those two capacities, the former president, who never hid his support from the beginning as he believed that it was the turn of the South East to produce the next leader in Nigeria and that Obi was the right man to do the job, not only donated his physical presence making some cameo appearances here and there in support of the ambition but finally cleared all doubt on January 1, 2023.

In a New Year message, which he personally signed, he said:

None of the contestants is a saint, but when one compares their character, antecedent, their understanding, knowledge, discipline, and vitality that they can bring to bear and the great efforts required to stay focused on the job, particularly looking at where the country is today and with the experience on the job that I personally had, Peter Obi, as a mentee, has an edge... One other important point to make about Peter is that he is a needle with thread attached to it from North and South and he may not get lost.

The result of all these was instant and quite remarkable. On the evening of February 25, 2023, Nigeria was practically raving. From North to the South, East, and West, the nation was in celebration mode. It was akin to the evening of June 12, 1993, when Nigerians felt they had turned the bend to face the boulevard of grand opportunities for the future. Yes, they had faced some hiccups during the day, but regardless, the results in their hands were enough to roll out the drums.

Aided by technology, which enabled them to record the results at polling stations in real-time they were sure of victory. From Lagos to Abeokuta, Ibadan to Osogbo; from Benue to Plateau to Nasarawa; from Benin to Uyo to Calabar; from Enugu to Owerri to Umuahia; from Kaduna to Minna, Abuja to Maiduguri, the picture of jubilating crowds of youths celebrating victory were posted all over social media. The mantra of *Eluu Pee* – a corruption of LP (Labour Party), echoed everywhere, depicting the counting at the polling stations.

Then, like 30 years ago when the June 12 saga unfolded, gloom enveloped the nation once again. The nation was practically hit by a thunderclap. Right before their eyes, another episode began to unravel. Their apprehension when the INEC IReV went kaput for the presidential election results, began to turn to reality. By the time night turned into day on February 26, it became clear that the worst had happened. Nigerians had lost once more.

Like the destruction of June 12, the country marked yet another descent through what Fela aptly described as "government magic." Blue began to turn to red and black to white. The imprimatur of entrenched interests was everywhere. Outrage! Nigerians cried! Nigerians remonstrated! They swore, vowed, and threatened. But no one listened. Like it was in the past, the nation had again been captured. Buhari had done his worst. It was the last of his gifts to Nigeria – the anti-climax of his disastrous presidency.

Of course, he had the willing tools at his beck and call. Prominent among them was INEC and the judiciary.

INEC: THE PARTICIPANT UMPIRE

Let me share a personal story as background to my concept of what a credible election should look like and the role institutions like INEC must play in making it so. On December 9, 2008, I was one of the journalists from across the world, who sat on the floor at the Electoral Commission of Ghana (ECG), to witness the announcement of the result of that year's presidential election in the country.

That event actually signified the end of about two days of tension-soaking political activities that accompanied the election. It was such a large crowd inside the equally spacious ECG hall that many could not find a space and had to make do with what was available, the floor. From outside, the din from the drumming, singing, and dancing of the supporters of the two major political gladiators, was seeping through, as we all waited with bated breath to witness what would happen.

The tension had been bolstered earlier in the several preceding hours following allegations and counter-allegations of rigging by the political gladiators. There had been press conferences where issues were joined by both the New Patriotic Front (NPP), the then ruling party, and the National Democratic Congress (NDC), from which it snatched power eight years before. That, of course, also informed the agitation outside party solidarity.

A wave of emotions and a tempestuous sensation ran through me immediately I heard the last words from Kwado Afari-Gyan, then Chairman of the ECG. I could have swallowed a fly without knowing as my mouth was thrown wide open in surprise. Did I hear that this man had just declared the election inconclusive? Did I just hear him order a runoff? Of course, I had heard of Ghana and the credibility of their electoral process after the surgical operation Jerry Rawlings, their late President, did to their national psyche. But I was never prepared for what I saw with my own eyes or heard with my ears.

In the election result he had just announced, Nana Akufo-Addo, candidate of the ruling NPP, had polled 4,159,439 or 49.13 per cent of the votes to beat Attah Millis, his NDC counterpart, who polled 4,056,634 or 47.92 per cent. The Ghanaian electoral laws stipulate that a candidate must score a little above 50 per cent of the votes cast to be declared the winner. In other words, all Akufo-Addo needed to be declared winner was just about one per cent of the votes to make a threshold of 51 per cent or thereabouts. Yet, Afari-Gyan, the ECG Chairman - conservative, urbane, haughty, austere, sterile – call him what you would – did not give it. It did not matter to him that this was the party of John Kufuor, the President in power at the time. He did not even bat an eyelid in making the decision.

That was my first shock. My mind went back to Nigeria, which had its own presidential election a year before that produced the late Umaru Yar'Adua, and how the PDP of then President Olusegun Obasanjo's government, practically broke the door with its feet in order to bulldoze its way to install the government. It was such a flawed election that even Yar'Adua, the main beneficiary, was too scandalised to accept it completely without offering his self-redeeming confession by not only attesting to its rottenness but offering immediate reforms.

How could a whole ruling party be that close to victory, only to be denied, when elsewhere in many African countries, where elections are mere formalities, votes are manufactured from anywhere to make up for the favoured candidates? My mind instantly raced to other countries outside Nigeria. What would have been the case in Zimbabwe under Robert Mugabe, Paul Biya in Cameroon, or Yoweri Museveni of Uganda?

This could not be happening in Africa, I told myself. I could also see the puzzlement on the faces of the oyibo journalists from foreign countries. Obviously, they must have become so used to issues of flawed elections in Africa that they were completely astounded by the development, wondering what was happening particularly when they had come armed to report bad news, as they are wont.

But there were more intrigues, if not shocks. That evening, I found myself in the home of Akufo-Addo. I wanted to know how he would react to the development. I had expected him, as the candidate of the ruling party, to be huffing and puffing in arrogance as a government baby. I expected him to be boastful about victory at the next edition – the rerun. However, the man I met was sober and prudent in his attitude to the entire development. His answer, when I asked him of the prospect of winning the rerun including the outstanding election in Tain constituency in Brand Aghafo region, was clear without equivocation.

He simply told me that he was aware that Ghanaians, having

voted the NPP on two previous occasions and after eight years, were already weary of continuing with the party and that there might be a gang-up with the other parties coalescing with the main opposition to back Mills. He was that plain if not audacious.

You know what? That was exactly how it turned out. The late President, at the second ballot, polled a total of 4,521,032 or 50.23 per cent, while Akufo-Addo, now President, polled 4,480,446 or 49.77 per cent to lose the election. Mills became the President on the strength of the predicted gang-up and coalition.

More interesting was the total absence of government interference in the matter. Kufuor did not even lift a finger to help his own party, neither did Akufo-Addo make a single reference to the President or any political superstructure during the encounter. It was simply a matter of the people of Ghana, their votes, and how they would use them. No more, no less!

Ironically, that night after the meeting with the NPP candidate, news filtered in that a powerful delegation from the Nigerian government had actually stormed the country to mount pressure on the president to twist the arms of the ECG boss to skew the election in Akufo-Addo's favour.

I had no way of confirming its veracity. But whether true or not, my Ghanaian journalist friends I was with in my hotel simply wanted to rub the message in, one of them went on to emphasise that it was a waste of time. They were sure that the President could not dare throw his weight around even if he wanted to. Afari-Gyan was as solid as the rock of Gibraltar, as constant as the Northern star, and as clean and straight as a pin. They were that sure about the integrity of the ECG boss.

Now, picture the two scenarios. Imagine a candidate of a ruling party in Nigeria needing just one per cent of the votes cast in an election to be declared president. Consider also that the candidate of the same party would be candid enough to admit that he could actually lose based on the feelings of the people. Who would have thought that a President of a ruling party would not pull the strings to practically install his successor no matter the odds, as was the case in 2007 and now 2023 in Nigeria?

That incident some years ago, has become my benchmark for measuring the credibility of other elections in Africa, particularly in Nigeria. Unfortunately, if any election has met that threshold, it is certainly not in Nigeria. Even the much-advertised 2015 election conducted by Attahiru Jega that brought in Buhari, was too fraught with many eerie revelations to come close to what I saw in Ghana.

The closest Nigeria could have gotten to that 2008 electoral feat in Ghana, would have been in the 2023 presidential polls. Everything was tapering towards that outcome until the unseen hands of evil got to work using the same Mahmood Yakubu, the selfsame INEC boss, who had given Nigeria such great hope, to deflate the balloon just at the final point.

To say that, like many other Nigerians, I was scandalised by the shocking outing of INEC is a clear understatement. I was completely gutted – shattered – wrecked, because the reality that I had been building the proverbial castle in the air, hit me like nothing else. Again, it had the trappings of Abiola's June 12 election. Let me even give a bit of background with my first encounter with the INEC boss. In 2021, a few months before the Anambra State governorship election, I was among the about 100 senior journalists that met with Mahmood in Lagos. It was an interaction with members of the Guild of Corporate Online Publishers (GOCOP). It was almost a daylong event of an admixture of serious and relaxed interactions.

Throughout the encounter, I kept looking for the tell-tale signs that would give him away as yet another of Nigeria's electoral dud cheques. Of course, he would not be the first electoral umpire I had met. I had actually interacted with virtually all his predecessors, right from President Ibrahim Babangida's June 12 era till date. In each case, it did not take too long before the nickel dropped for them to give themselves away as working for some established interests.

In fact, Yakubu's countenance actually betrayed some of the traits of Afari-Gyan, the Ghanaian ECG boss. It was at that forum that he provided the details of the Bimodal Voters Accreditation System (BVAS) and the INEC Result Viewing (IReV) portal. At that parley, each of the departmental heads was given the opportunity to brief the audience on the relevance of their functions towards the ultimate goal of election credibility.

Chidi Nwafor, the Director of Information Communication Technology (ICT), was very clinical in his presentation at that forum on the BVAS and IReV technology on which the gamut of the process and expectation of clean elections was hinged. In the end, he told his audience that the mechanism, which was first tested in the Nasarawa Central by-election a few months back, was so tamperproof and airtight that it would not even allow air to seep through, not to talk about leaking water. He was that confident. Why not? After all, he was said to have built the system from scratch and had already test-run it to authenticate its dependability.

To every doubt, he offered the same confident assurance – nothing would go wrong. Pressed further that this was technology, which could never be 100 per cent foolproof, he countered that not in this case. In fact, his charge to the about 100 members of GOCOP was to watch out for the wonders of the system. Then Anambra happened. The November 2012 governorship election that produced Chukwuma Soludo was so seamless that none of the candidates who lost considered the legal option to contest the outcome. Though the Ekiti and Osun in June and July of 2022 witnessed legal challenges, the reputation of the BVAS and IReV was already very much established. Nigerians knew that there was a new sheriff in town in terms of credible elections.

That was the confidence with which they approached the 2023 general election. But who was to know that Mahmood and his INEC had something up their sleeve and were going to change the goalpost in the middle of the match to produce the disaster which the exercise eventually turned out to be? At the last count, the election which initially held the hope that Nigeria had eventually turned the bend and was on the way to taking its rightful place not only as the pride of Africa but as a global power in its own right turned out the direct opposite. Hope again had been dashed as it was in virtually all previous exercises.

INEC had identified 10 major problems the introduction of the BVAS and IReV were supposed to solve - falsification of votes at polling units, falsification of the number of accredited voters, collation of false results, swapping of result sheets, forging of result sheets, snatching and destruction of result sheets, mutilation of false results, computational errors, obtaining declaration and return involuntarily, premature declaration and return while collation is ongoing, and poor record-keeping.

It was almost at the threshold of achieving the above milestones at the point of the February 25 election. But by that singular act of shutting down the IReV and ensuring that its officials were not able to post the results of the presidential elections, INEC effectively slammed the door in the face of Nigeria. It was an abrupt end to national hope. It was like firing a shot at the huge balloon which began to inflate with the signing into law of the 2022 electoral Act which sanctioned electronic voting or the Nigerian version of it, which by then seemed to have set sail thereafter. The balloon did not only deflate, it shattered completely.

By that action, it was back to the manual system, meaning the process was effectively handed back to the politicians who knew what to do. Within hours after the presidential election, the INEC staff, who were either intimidated or besieged with hefty financial and other inducements, willingly acquiesced, practically abandoning the process. Videos actually caught some of them making feeble efforts in protest as the foot-soldiers of the APC went to work to cook the electoral books where they desired and in the manner they deemed fit.

Do not be deceived by the distribution of the votes to create the impression that the candidates won where they were strong. It was the job of the smart alecs, that handled the APC rigging machine. Those in charge ensured that they did not go for the total kill as a strategy to avoid the similar scenario of the landslide victory era of the Second Republic or breaking the door tactics of the PDP. All they needed was just to be declared the winner, and that is what they got.

Babachel Lawal, former Secretary to the Government of the Federation (SGF) in Buhari's government, was one of those who cried blue murder over the development. One of the big wigs from the North, the former SGF, was one of the virulent voices that kicked against the Muslim-Muslim ticket Tinubu ran with Kashim Shettima, his running mate, now the Vice President. He was no less so, in his assessment of the outcome of the election, all but dismissing it as a fraud. His analogy was that knowing he would not win the election, Tinubu prepared merely prepared to capture the process, while his opponents were preparing for the election.

In a widely circulated statement on Tuesday, October 17, 2023, he wrote:

I have resisted the temptation to engage in the contemporary political discourse since the February 2023 election faux pas.

I did this for two reasons; the first being that as an active player in the drama, I needed time to analyze and digest the data that led to the outcome(s) so I could arrive at an informed decision; the second being that the rainy season had just set in and it was necessary that I focused my attention on my farms which are the mainstay of my livelihood.

The current topical issues for political discourse and inquiry are whether or not Bola Tinubu won the presidential election and/or that he was a priori qualified to participate in the election given his murky bio data as is now being publicly unveiled daily in an avalanche.

My answer to the first inquiry is that regardless of whatever INEC or Appeal Court said or did, Bola did not win the election. Right from the start of the campaigns, Bola knew he was not going to win the election in a free and fair contest, so he decided to go by all means.

Available factual data, as aggregated from several independent sources, indicate that Obi got the majority votes while Atiku came second. Bola came a distant third in the number of votes scored.

This, to many, is exactly the correct reading of the trajectory that birthed Tinubu's arrival at the Aso Rock Presidential Villa in Abuja. It was the handiwork of an INEC and Mahmood Yakubu who decided to be players in a game they were officiating.

One sticky point, which INEC has failed to extricate itself from, is the distrust arising from the sudden redeployment of Chidi Nwafor, Director of the ICT outside the commission's headquarters in Abuja, far from his area of core competency into obscurity. What was the hurry that such a critical component of the commission would be touched at such a critical time, let alone, the man, who was responsible for its top-notch transformation? Till date, nobody has come with any credible, convincing answers.

All INEC's best attempts to make the world believe that it was a routine measure, have remained futile. Few people are convinced. How could the world be convinced that redeploying the man reputed to have built the BVAS and IReV from scratch, to Enugu on August 16, 2022, six months before the crucial election as an Administrative Secretary, and replacing him, with at best, a rookie, had no ulterior motive? Even an imbecile would not buy into it, especially with the way the result turned out eventually. Explaining away the action, has been like a stubborn bone stuck to the throat of the commission.

Why would INEC remove such a key officer at the time it mattered most, especially for an election whose integrity is reliant on ICT almost completely? This was a man that was so good at his work that he was hired by the Liberian Electoral Commission

(LEC) and did so well that he became the toast of not only the entire commission, but the entire country and even the Economic Community of West African States (ECOWAS). Who would blame anyone who believes that the *Technical Glitch* INEC blamed for the failure of the IReV, flowed from this specific development as a grand plot to derail the process?

JUDICIARY: JUDGEMENTS WITHOUT JUSTICE

The issue of the judiciary as it relates to the presidential election of 2023 is, in itself, another ugly side to the entire odious and macabre story. But first, another background! About one and a half years after the assumption of power by Buhari, the nation woke up with the shocking news that different squads of the Department of State Services (DSS), had stormed the homes of Nigerian judges in the wee hours of Saturday, October 8, 2016. Details of the invasion suggested some macabre images. Some of the judges were virtually pulled out of their beds in their underpants and others completely in their birthday suits, with their spouses to boot.

The raids, were said to have been carried out simultaneously in Abuja, Port Harcourt, Gombe, Kano, Enugu, and Sokoto. The reason the secret police gave for the strange operation was linking their lordships to some questionable financial transactions. The eerie onslaught, was the first time such would happen in Nigeria. In fact, it is said that some of the victims of that nightmare, are still unable to get out of the trauma of that night. Prominent among them, were Sylvester Ngwuta and John Okoro, both of the Supreme Court, as well as Adeniyi Ademola and Nnamdi Dimgba of the Federal High Court in Abuja.

The residence of Kabiru Auta, a High Court judge in Kano, was also raided along with that of Innocent Umezuluike, retired chief judge of Enugu State, both earlier recommended for retirement by the Nigerian Judicial Council (NJC), the body for the reward and punishment of judges in Nigeria, in addition to Muazu Pindiga, Gombe State judge.

Muhammed Liman, a Federal High Court judge in Port Harcourt, was saved the same ordeal by Nyesom Wike, then Governor of Rivers State, who personally took charge of the situation through his physical presence at the number 35 Force Avenue residence of the judge in the state capital. He practically stopped the DSS officials from conducting what he called an act of impunity, which he swore would not happen under his watch.

Now the explanation from the government, was that the raid was in line with Buhari's anti-corruption crusade. But, even at that early stage, when Nigerians still had some modicums of trust in the government's anti-corruption thrust, not a few saw this completely outlandish behaviour of invading the houses of judges as going beyond that official explanation. Those who were bold enough, clearly gave it a name – intimidation of the judiciary.

Till date, not a few Nigerians are still waiting for the moment the judges would be led away to jail, given the slew of allegations and the heaps of evidence those who carried out the operations, were said to have discovered. Nothing of the sort has happened. It is not likely to happen because the objective, seems to have since been accomplished. It was a mission to scare the judges, show them who the master is and whip them into line. None of the judges was ever jailed as a result. In fact, beyond the torments and tribulations they faced on the night of that invasion, the issues of the cases against them were subsumed in judicial masturbations until they were struck out one after the other.

But not the impact. Now, what is left is perhaps the intended clear message – you are no longer untouchables. Or in the way Nigerians would put it – if you do anyhow, you see anyhow. Is it not strange that no court has ruled against the Federal Government ever since, especially in high-profile cases, where they have substantial interest? Not even split decisions are available now. All you hear today are unanimous judgements, suggesting judges are apparently so cowed that none wants to be noticed stepping outside the prescribed lines to annoy the powers that be. Of course, a child stung by a bee becomes wary of the housefly.

If the invasion of judges' homes, was not convincing enough the Onnoghen saga, presented an extra proof of government's obvious red eyes. On January 12, 2018, the news broke that the Code of Conduct Bureau (CCB), had filed a six-count charge against Walter Onnoghen, then Chief Justice of Nigeria (CJN). It came via a petition launched by Anti-Corruption and Research-Based Data Initiative (ARDI), a hitherto unknown entity, but linked to Buhari, to the CCB. The allegation was that the then CJN did not declare his assets.

The group led by one Denis Aghanya, said Onnoghen, who assumed office as CJN on March 6, 2017, a few months after the invasion of judges' homes, *is the owner of sundry accounts primarily funded through cash deposits made by himself up to as recently as 10th August 2016, which appear to have been run in a manner inconsistent with financial transparency and the code of conduct for public officials.*

Specifically, the group said the CJN made five different cash deposits of $10,000 each on March 8, 2011, into Standard Chartered Bank Account 1062650; two separate cash deposits of $5,000 each, followed by four cash deposits of $10,000 each on June 7, 2011; another set of five separate cash deposits of $10,000 each on June 27, 2011, and four more cash deposits of $10,000 each the following day.

Alleging that he did not declare his assets immediately after taking office, contrary to Section 15 (1) of the Code of Conduct Bureau and Tribunal Act; and that he did not comply with the constitutional requirement for public servants to declare their assets every four years during their career, Aghanya and his men also alleged that Onnoghen's Code of Conduct Bureau Forms (Form CCB 1) for 2014 and 2016, were dated and filed on the same day and the acknowledgment slips, were issued for both on December 14, 2016 — at which point they said he had become the CJN.

They also said he appeared to have suppressed or otherwise concealed the existence of these multiple domiciliary accounts owned by him, as well as the substantial cash balances in them adding:

It is curious that these domiciliary accounts were not declared in one of the two CCB Forms filed by Justice Onnoghen on the same day, 14th December 2016.

We believe our petition has established cases of suspicious financial and other transactions against His Lordship, collusion between His Lordship and various banks related to Suspicious Transactions Reporting (STR) and financial transactions not justifiable by His Lordship's lawful remuneration at all material times.

The circus decked in a sumptuous dose of melodrama and tragicomedy, then, progressed in quick succession. While Nigerians were still grasping with the headlines, the CCB on January 12 announced that it had filed a six-count charge against the CJN. Two days later, the trial began on January 14. Then Buhari, who had earlier ordered Onnoghen to step aside on January 22, follow up with his suspension from office three days later on January 25, and went ahead to replace him with Justice Ibrahim Tanko on the same day. The swiftness with which these events progressed and particularly with Buhari, who had built an uncanny reputation for his prevarication and laid-back model of dealing with officials, even the most indolent of them, now acting with jet-like speed, did not go unnoticed, neither the unpronounced, but inferred intent.

Even the international community could not maintain its diplomatic reticence as the tapes rolled in the outlandish drama with all the lurid details. A few hours after the Buhari hammer, the US and the EU joined the voices of Nigerians in crying blue murder. Washington reacted through its embassy in Abuja, condemning the move, which many critics believed was targeted at the coming presidential election.

US-Abuja wrote:

The Embassy of the United States is deeply concerned by the impact of the executive branch's decision to suspend and replace the Chief Justice and head of the judicial branch without the support of the legislative branch on the eve of national and state elections.

We note widespread Nigerian criticism that this decision is unconstitutional and that it undermines the independence of the judicial branch. That undercuts the stated determination of government, candidates, and political party leaders to ensure that the elections proceed in a way that is free, fair, transparent and peaceful – leading to a credible result.

We urge that the issues raised by this decision be resolved swiftly and peacefully in accordance with due process, full respect for the rule of law, and the spirit of the Constitution of Nigeria. Such action is needed urgently now to ensure that this decision does not cast a pall over the electoral process.

The EU, which followed suit swiftly, was even more direct in connecting the dots by linking the move to the election. It wrote:

The European Union was invited by the Independent National Electoral Commission to observe the 2019 general elections.

The EU Election Observation Mission (EU EOM) is very concerned about the process and timing of the suspension of the Chief Justice of Nigeria, Honourable Justice Walter Onnoghen, on 25 January.

With 20 days until the presidential and National Assembly elections, political parties, candidates, and voters must be able to have confidence in the impartiality and independence of the judicial system.

The decision to suspend the Chief Justice has led to many Nigerians, including lawyers and civil society observer groups, to question whether due process was followed. The timing, just before the swearing-in of justices for Electoral Tribunals and the hearing of election-related cases, has also raised concerns about the opportunity for electoral justice.

The EU EOM calls on all parties to follow the legal processes provided for in the Constitution and to respond calmly to any concerns they may have. The EU EOM will continue observing all aspects of the election, including the independence of the election administration, the neutrality of security agencies, and the extent to which the judiciary can and does fulfil its election-related responsibilities.

Naturally, the response from Buhari was expected:

Nigeria reserves the right to be insulated from suggestions and or interference with respect to wholly internal affairs and commends international laws, customs and norms that mandate and require nations and the comity to respect this prerogative to all.

Nigeria is confident of its electoral processes and her preparation for the imminent elections, and the federal government has supported the independent electoral umpire in both its independence and resources needed to accomplish our desire and insistence on free and fair elections.

In addition, the Federal government has ensured the independence of all organs, institutions and arms of government to perform their functions in a manner that is transparent and is not lacking in integrity whether institutionally or by persons within such institutions or organs and will continue to do this.

Although the question of foreign interference, whether state sponsored, promoted or otherwise, has dominated recent elections and outcomes globally, the federal government assures citizens and the global community that it will fiercely and assiduously promote the will and the right of Nigerians to choose and elect their leaders without pressure or assistance from persons or entities that are not constitutionally empowered to participate in the process, wrote Garba Shehu, Buhari's spokesman, in quick riposte on January 27.

By the time the February 23, 2019, presidential election was concluded and the final words on the electoral disputes were pronounced by the Supreme Court on October 30 of that year, those who saw the hands of Esau and heard the voice of Jacob in the entire judicial saga from the invasion of the homes of judges to the removal of Onnoghen confirmed their worst fears. Their conclusion was that the judiciary, had, apart from being hard-done-by – was now completely ensnared.

Even after the Onnoghen episode, the APC government, apparently discovering its potency, especially having carried out this unholy strategy unchallenged, had continued with the trajectory. Another chapter suggested that there were more in the bag of intrigues! On June 22, 2022, few months to the 2023 presidential elections, Justice Ibrahim Tanko, Onnoghen's replacement, suddenly resigned his office. The abruptness of his action, naturally activated the public antenna once again. The official explanation, of course, was that the CJN was managing a fragile health condition, which would be too heavy for his duties. But, that tale was only too familiar. The naysayers, who thumbed their noses at the explanation, believing there was more to it, waited for details.

In time they started unfolding. It was reported that even the family members of the former CJN, were taken aback by the decision of their patriarch, as they did not see it coming, casting doubts on the health angle. Soon, reports began to highlight what seemed the real reason(s). One of them, was the massive pressure piling up at that moment, both within and outside against the jurist. From within, his colleagues at the Supreme Court, were agitating over issues bothering on their welfare.

Soon, the judiciary, a hitherto closed environment, shed its conservative nature to come under the intense exposure of the klieg light. On June 20, the Nigerian media were awash with a leaked letter of 14 justices of the Supreme Court confronting the CJN in a letter of protest, listing non-replacement of poor vehicles; accommodation problems; lack of drugs at the Supreme Court clinic; epileptic electricity supply to the Supreme Court premises; increase in electricity tariff; no increase in the allowances for diesel; lack of Internet services to residences and chambers; and poor take-home pay that could no longer take them halfway as part of their complaints. Again, it was the first time the conservative institution of the judiciary would open its bowel to such public scrutiny.

Even the ex-CJN, was taken aback by the development. In his clapback, he not only accused his colleagues of stabbing him in the back by leaking the letter to the media, but in a statement signed by Ahuraka Yusuf Isah, his spokesman, wondered when issues concerning the judiciary became a matter for public consumption, rather than the private matter that ought to be discussed among 'brothers.'

He wrote:

The Chief Justice of Nigeria, Hon Justice Ibrahim Tanko Mohammad, would wish to confirm receipt of a letter written and addressed to him by his brother Justices of the Supreme Court Bench. Judges in all climes are to be seen and not heard and that informed why the CJN refrained from joining issues until a letter said to be personal is spreading across the length and breadth of the society.

This was akin to dancing naked at the market square by us with the ripple effect of the said letter. The Supreme Court definitely does not exist outside its environment − it is also affected by the economic and socio-political climate prevailing in the country.

In addition to the heat from his colleagues, there were also reports of pressures from the NJC, the National Assembly, and the Presidency, each threatening to institute a probe, which all complicated the situation to make it too combustible for the ex-CJN to bear. Why the sudden pressure on the man appointed to replace Onnoghen? Why did his environment become so toxic so soon after?

Vanguard of June 30, 2022, in its report on the matter, quoted a presidential source as saying that the judiciary boss was even given the option of the carrot and the stick, stating:

Tanko was forced to sign the already prepared resignation letter honourably with a promise to be conferred with the second highest national honours or be given Justice Onnoghen treatment.

The Chief Justice of Nigeria, as he then was, had no option under the circumstance other than to append his signature to the document and bid the judiciary bye. The moment he tendered the letter, President Muhammadu Buhari, unlike his style, did not waste time to swear in the next most senior justice, Justice Olukayode Ariwoola, as the acting CJN at the Council Chambers of the State House, Abuja.

This report, if true, would again support another "conspiracy theory" of an ethnic hand being played, just like in the case of Onnoghen, where it was said that his removal had to do with Buhari not wanting to take the risk of a judiciary headed by someone from the South determining his fate in the 2019 election.

Remember that Yemi Osinbajo, former Vice President, standing in as acting President, had seen to the appointment and inauguration of Onnoghen at the expiration of the tenure of Mahmoud Mohammed, when Buhari was lying on his hospital bed in

London. Not a few had sworn that were the former President in office, Onnoghen, who assumed the office on the basis of seniority, would never have emerged regardless of his status.

So, in the ethnic slant that Tanko's ouster was similarly given, the convenient interpretation was that as Buhari ensured that his brother superintended over the judiciary that handled his, Tinubu, who had since emerged the candidate of the APC some weeks earlier, would settle for no less either. Therefore, a Yoruba man had to come in. The coming of Olukayode Ariwoola was therefore part of the setup, those pushing the narrative further advanced. Right or wrong, true or false, the jury is still out.

What is more? As if these supposed political intrigues and considerations at the judiciary high command were not enough, the pronouncement of judges added to the pile of garbage that enhanced the putrefaction. Result! Instead of smelling roses, the Nigerian judiciary currently oozes bad odour like an unattended public latrine. Instead of maintaining the acclaimed toga of the last hope of the oppressed, it has since become the least hope of the downtrodden.

Nothing points to this parlous situation than the cases of Godswill Akpabio and Ahmad Lawan. They are the locus classicus of the face of today's judiciary under the APC. The two cases take the trophy in showcasing the most bizarre and outlandish – the most glaring, brazen and demonstrable specimen of judicial abracadabra. Some details. The 2022 Electoral Act, to cure a debilitating political ailment of politicians jumping from one party to the other during primaries just to obtain tickets to contest elections, put a seal on that practice. It clearly stated that a politician that takes part in the primaries of one political party, is barred from participating in another. It also barred them from contesting for different positions in an election cycle.

Akpabio, former Governor of Akwa Ibom and a senator in the Ninth National Assembly, had resigned his position as minister of Niger Delta in the government of Buhari to contest against Tinubu in the APC primaries of June 7 and 8, 2022. On the other hand, Lawan, the Senate President, also threw his hat into the ring for the same contest. Both lost out. That should have put paid to their individual ambitions to contest for other offices under the said Act.

But what did Nigerians see? On Friday, January 20, 2023, the Supreme Court retrieved the mandate held by Udom Ekpoudom, retired Deputy Inspector General of Police (DIG), who actually contested and won the slot for the Akwa Ibom North-West Senatorial District at the time Akpabio was supposedly slugging it out with Tinubu in Abuja, and handed the same over to the former governor.

Even though the case was seen as provincial, the din from the general outrage echoed beyond Akwa Ibom to shake the collective psyche of many political watchers. Nothing seemed to them more outlandish. The media were practically set ablaze by the groundswell of the echoes of the bitter public discontent. But those who thought that the apex court would be circumscribed by the ear-splitting public outcries were disappointed. It was certainly not done yet.

On February 6, exactly 17 days after Akpabio, the same court did an encore. Lawan was declared the candidate of the Yobe North Senatorial District. The ticket was retrieved from Bashir Machina, who, like Ekpuodom, had won the ticket during the original primaries. The only mitigating factor in this case was, unlike the

Akwa Ibom edition, which came via a unanimous judgement read by Justice Ibrahim Saulawa, the judges in that of Lawan were split – two to three with the majority favouring the former Senate President. It was read by Justice Chima Centus Nweze.

But the effect was no less telling on Nigerians who watched in utter disbelief. For those who saw it as the height of judicial reck-lessness, if not iniquity, it was a mortal blow indicating a dan-gerous vibration at the pillars holding the temple of justice that could only lead to a fatal end – total collapse. For many still, the surprise was with Nweze. His involvement seemed to mimic that last cry of Julius Caesar when Marcus Brutus dealt him his own dagger-blow that finally killed his spirit and made him succumb to death – *et tu, Brute!*

How could the radical jurist lend himself to such a clear miscar-riage of justice? This was the popular question in the minds of the naysayers. If anyone could soil his hand with such, in their estimation, perverse judgement, certainly not the erudite jurist whose actions and words spoke for him right from his activist years as a lawyer in Enugu.

Perhaps a little on the dossier of the late JSC, as he then was! A native of Obollo, Udenu Local Government Area of Enugu State, Nweze, who was born on September 25, 1958, apart from being reputed to have had a sterling career, was seen as belonging to the class of fearless judges of recent Nigerian judicial history. In his about 30 years on the bench, which began after his appoint-ment from private practice as a lawyer in 1995, he was one of the judges who had promoted the doctrine that justice must be done even if the heavens fall.

One of the latest outings and demonstrable examples of this

was in 2020. He practically cried blue murder as he rebuffed and confronted his colleagues at the apex court in the case of Hope Uzodimma against Emeka Ihedioha, in the contest for Douglas House, home of the governor of Imo State. Yes! *The Imo State case!* Nigerians had woken up on Tuesday, January 14 of that year to the shocking and somewhat devastating news that the Supreme Court had removed Ihedioha, who originally came first in the governorship election of March 9, 2019, and replaced him with Uzodimma, who came a distant fourth in the same election.

To many, that development not only came as one of the most unbelievably odious judicial pronouncements in history but among the most classic examples of the rot in the judiciary – one that apparently dealt the heaviest and deadliest assaults to the country's temple of justice in decades.

When the matter returned to the same apex court for review, Nweze was the only one among the seven justices who emphasised this assessment by reversing himself and returning Ihedioha, the candidate of the PDP who was sworn in on May 29, 2019, and had therefore enjoyed power for seven months, while sacking Uzodimma of the APC. Not only did he reverse himself, he also admonished his colleagues to do the same, reminding them of posterity.

Hear him:

This decision of the Supreme Court will continue to haunt our electoral jurisprudence for a long time to come. This court has a duty of redeeming its image. It is against this background that the finality of the court cannot extinguish the right of any person. I am of the view that this application should succeed. I hereby make an order repealing the decision of this court made on Janu-

ary 14 and that the certificate of return issued to the appellant (Uzodinma) be returned to INEC. I also make an order restoring the respondent (Ihedioha) as the winner of the March 9, 2019 governorship election.

So, what happened that he could switch in such a manner so soon after? Many believe that he was like a lion on a leash that became powerless to the mockery and taunting of the lesser animals. In fact, that he was the one to read the lead-judgement was quite instructive, as there is the belief that it was a way of his supposed traducers proving their powers. It was their way of rubbing in the vulnerability of the late jurist in their powerful grip. They must have insisted that he did that job to prove a point.

Instead of the hitherto fearless jurist toeing the path he was known for, it was Justices Emmanuel Agim and Adamu Jauro that stood up against Lawan. In their dissenting judgements, they held that the former Senate President never participated in the APC primary held on May 28 as he withdrew voluntarily to participate in the presidential primary held on June 8, 2022, adding that the conduct of another primary on June 9, 2022, where Lawan emerged was in breach of Section 84 (5) of the Electoral Act as the APC never cancelled that held on May 28 before organising another.

Unfortunately, there is no way of knowing if Nweze acted independently or under a leash. He died on Sunday, July 30, 2022, completing about eight years on the apex court bench, having been appointed by former President Goodluck Jonathan in 2014 from the Court of Appeal, where he was elevated to in 2008 from the Enugu State High Court. An account has it that he died a broken man because he could not live with the consequential harm of that Yobe outing. The serious blemish on his otherwise blistering career obviously quickened his death. Apart from this, his fate was reportedly sealed when, in addition to his battle with his health challenges, which deteriorated after that judgement, he was also allegedly denied a visa to travel to the US to attend to his health. Today, both Akpabio and Lawan are in the Senate. For Akpabio, it is even more. He is now the Senate President. What a way of passing a judgement on not only the judiciary, what a way of situating the Nigerian democracy!

So, when the mantra – *go to court* – began reverberating everywhere after the 2023 elections, especially from the victorious APC elements, INEC, as well as officials of the Buhari government, even the imbeciles among the many watchers of the unfolding scenario, could not help but detect the buoying confidence imbedded in that song. Yet for many, the electoral infamy was just too much for any court to ignore.

So, amid the heavy despondency in the polity, many still harboured the hope that somehow the judiciary would come to the rescue. After all, the judges themselves were Nigerians imbued with nationalistic fervour to liberate the country, beyond the divine calling as arbiters in the temple of justice.

It is important to travel this route to establish the rating of the Nigerian judiciary that sat on the case of Obi and to another extent – Atiku. It is important to indicate what many people thought about the institution even before the former governor went there. Not a few Nigerians were convinced that the move would be futile. I was among those who believed that it would take a miracle for the election results to be upturned and Obi given victory despite my belief that he clearly and thunderously won the election. Why? My position was strengthened by historical judicial trajectory. Nobody from the First Republic, the Second

Republic, and the current democratic experiment that started in 1999, had been able to achieve the feat of upturning a presidential election no matter the weight of evidence supporting him.

Obafemi Awolowo never did against Shehu Shagari in 1979, despite what the picture showed in that election. In fact, the twelve-two-thirds of 19 states declaration of the Supreme Court in that case is still hanging in the throat of the nation's jurisprudence, as a reference point of the Awolowo-Shagari debacle. Olu Falae, despite the thinking of many that he trounced Olusegun Obasanjo in 1999, is still licking his wounds together with his supporters to date.

Before he eventually became victorious in 2015, the belief in many quarters was that Buhari was not only robbed at the polls but at the tribunals, particularly in 2003 and 2007. The best he got out of his judicial efforts, was in 2003, when the late Justice Sylvanus Nsofor, gave a dissenting judgement in his favour nullifying the election of Obasanjo.

Reviewing that election, he had declared:

I find that the substantial non-compliance with the mandatory electoral law amounts to no election. I also find that there was violence perpetrated by President Obasanjo...May Nigeria never and never again see a Black Saturday like April 19, 2003.

In fact, the best bet I had hoped was that there could be one or two Nsofors in the Tinubu case, who might act as loose cannons among his panel either at the PEPT acting as the Appeal Court or at the Supreme Court. That dream was never to be, however. That happening, could have been the elixir that would have helped Nigerians to breathe in the lingering hope that the judiciary could somehow, be salvaged. It never came to pass.

Besides, anyone with his head on his shoulder, who either watched the body language or heard the pronouncements of the APC camp, including Buhari and his men, would come to the conclusion that the judicial angle had since been covered and therefore it was a waste of time. It was like Ibrahim Babangida in his heyday as military President declaring – *we are not only in office, we are in power.* It was that obvious.

In the first effort, the Presidential Election Petition Tribunal (PEPT), acting as the court of first instance in presidential election matters, had consolidated the petitions of Obi, Atiku, and Allied Peoples Movement (APM), the only other political party that contested Tinubu's declaration as winner of the 2023 polls by INEC, because all the prayers were similar.

The pillars of the petitions actually centred on the contention that Tinubu did not win the lawful votes cast in the election and that INEC abandoning the use of IReV to transmit results in real-time dealt a fatal blow to the exercise, hence it ought to be cancelled.

There was also the question of the non-qualification of Tinubu to contest the election in the first place, based on different contentions, including forgery as a result of the claim by the former Lagos State Governor that he attended Chicago State University, which Atiku claimed was false; double nomination of Kashim Shettima, his running mate, accused of not resigning as a candidate for Borno Central Senatorial seat before picking up his nomination for the VP position.

There were also issues around his educational background, given that his only deposition at INEC, was that he attended Chicago State University, while the slots for primary and secondary schools attended were reportedly left blank, a development his traducers believed amounted to perjury.

Again, they also raised the issue of his alleged conviction in the US for drug offences based on his forfeiture of $460,000 to avoid prosecution, in addition to submitting that by virtue of his not scoring 25 per cent of the votes in the Federal Capital Territory (FCT), INEC should not have declared him winner.

In the main, the parties asked for an order cancelling the election and compelling the INEC to conduct a fresh election at which Tinubu and APC would not participate. The petitioners had waited for the PEPT to make clear pronouncements on these headline demands, which were in fact a distillation of the gamut of issues they had with the exercise. They were not the only ones who waited. Nigeria waited with them with bated breath as well.

Then on the morning of September 6, 2023, the voice of Justice Haruna Tsammani, who led the five-man panel of the PEPT, booming with authority in the airwaves across the country, ended with a note of finality:

This petition accordingly lacks merit. I affirm the return of Bola Ahmed Tinubu as the duly elected President of the Federal Republic of Nigeria. The parties are to bear their costs.

To underscore the fact that he was not alone, he passed the microphone to each of the remaining four justices on the bench with him, who equally added their corroborative voices. Earlier, the world – for the election was not only a Nigerian event but evoked the interest of the global audience – had watched as he destroyed each of the pillars on which the hope of those who had feared the worst but hoped for the best stood.

One after the other, he broke each supporting bone. And as the people heard the sound of each cracking, it sent shockwaves in their own collective anatomy. They winced as they heard him dismiss the insistence of the petitioners that the 2022 Electoral Act made electronic transfer of results to IReV mandatory with these words: *There is no provision for the electronic transmission of election results in the Electoral Act 2022. It is at best optional.* An option?! Now this was the same mechanism INEC went around the world, including the Chatham House in the United Kingdom, trumpeting as the game changer – the same document on which the credibility and integrity of the election was built. Now an option?

For emphasis on this, hear Yakubu speak on Wednesday, February 22, 2023, exactly three days to the election:

The BVAS confirms that the cards issued by the commission and presented by the voter are genuine and the voter is authenticated using the fingerprint and where it failed, the facial. Where both fail, the voter can't vote. That is a matter of law. After the process is completed at the polling unit, the image of the polling unit result will be taken by the BVAS and uploaded into what we call the INEC Result Viewing Portal where citizens can see polling unit level results as the processes are completed at polling unit level.

In fact, the INEC boss, still assuring Nigerians about the foolproof nature of the process and the readiness to keep it so, stressed that it was for this reason that the commission decided to use images rather than transmitting raw results, unlike the case of Kenya, another African country which successfully held a fully electronic-based election, which Nigeria was trying to mimic.

Hear him again:

The difference between what Kenya did in 2015 and what we are doing is that we are not transmitting raw figures for collation. In fact, the law does not allow for electronic collation of results. So, we don't transmit raw figures because raw figures transmitted online are more susceptible to hacking while images of a document are not susceptible to hacking.

Again, as the voice of the erudite jurist boomed, the world heard him loud and clear, saying that there was no evidence that Tinubu's forfeiture of $460,000, was a criminal offence as there was no trial to that effect, not to talk about conviction to warrant his disqualification as a candidate in the presidential polls. The PEPT had equally dismissed the case of double nomination that would have led to disqualification on the ground that being a pre-election matter, it ought to have begun at the Federal High Court.

But, remember that in a separate case, the same Supreme Court had upheld the judgements of the Court of Appeal which endorsed that of the Federal High Court that the PDP, which instituted the same case insisting on the dissolution of the Tinubu ticket based on double nomination, was a busy body and meddlesome interloper because it was a matter of the APC's internal affairs.

On May 26, 2023, Justice Adamu Jauro, reading the unanimous judgement of the apex court, had said:

The position of the law has always been that no political party can challenge the nomination of a candidate of another political party. The position did not change in section 285(14)(c) of the constitution. No matter how pained or disgruntled a political party is with the way and manner another political party is con-

ducting or has conducted its affairs concerning its nomination of candidates for any position, it must keep mum and remain an onlooker for he lacks locus standi to challenge such nomination in court. Section 285(14)(c) of the constitution only allows a political party to challenge the decisions and activities of INEC disqualifying its own candidate from participating in an election.

So, head or tail – through the regular courts or PEPT, the petitioners failed. The rest of the world would probably have shaken their heads in wonderment, while many Nigerians directly hit by the impact of the pronouncements, went to bed with fever, not knowing how to handle their disappointment. But they moved on. Yes! This road is closed, but surely not all the roads.

Therefore, as the petitioners moved to the next stage, they followed, believing that somehow something – the judicial miracle they had hoped and prayed for – would happen. At the Supreme Court, events even got grittier, much more so. By this time, the Atiku camp had upped the ante in the damning issue over Tinubu's claim that he attended Chicago State University after his forgery case was killed at the PEPT.

The din arising from this move for days and weeks on end, was so deafening, just as the drama was so captivating to the extent that little else seemed to engage the time and interest of Nigerians and those watching across the globe. As the supposed can of worms spilled its content, or so it was canvassed, including that the certificate Tinubu was claiming from the institution actually belonged to a female and that the Lagos State Government College where he allegedly claimed to have obtained the entry certificate to apply for admission into the university in 1970, was actually established in 1974, Nigerians and their supporters on the other side of the divide, were sure this was the clincher.

The din this time was even louder than the issue of the $460,000 forfeiture discovery. It was a loud, collective shout of *Eureka!* This time, he has been cornered and there would be no room to escape. Of course, there was. In fact, Atiku obviously wasted his time, efforts and money as it were. The Supreme Court did not even look at the matter at all as it flung the package it came with out of the window.

Justice Nyang Okoro, leading a seven-man panel of the Supreme Court to deliver the final judgement on October 26, was quite emphatic. He held that Atiku was already too late as he ought to have brought the issue before the PEPT, and having not done so at the lower court, the hands of the apex court were tied. It would not listen to him.

Two days earlier, when they first heard the matter, Chris Uche (SAN), Atiku's lawyer, had laboured very intensively, pleading with him and his panel to admit the document in evidence, citing the implication of a person so smeared with such damning content, being the President of Nigeria, particularly the image it would portray within and outside Nigeria.

He argued:

The issue involving Tinubu's certificate is a weighty, grave, and constitutional one which the Supreme Court should admit. I urge the court to admit the fresh evidence of President Tinubu's academic records from CSU presented by Atiku. The court should take a look at Tinubu's records and reach a decision devoid of technicality. As a policy court, the court has a duty to look at it and should side-step technicalities.

No dice! In fact, during that hearing on October 24, Okoro and his colleagues had on their own, even before adjourning the matter indefinitely, tried to shoot down the evidence by emphasising that being a criminal matter, the allegation ought to be proved beyond reasonable doubt. In his words:

This is a criminal matter that has to be proved beyond reasonable doubt. There are two conflicting letters from the CSU: one authenticating the president's certificate and another discrediting it.

Emmanuel Agim, who was also on the panel, was even sharper, pointing out that the CSU deposition Atiku was seeking to tender as evidence was done in the chambers of Atiku's lawyer and not in the courtroom, adding:

I expected the college to write disclaiming the documents in dispute. Does a stenographer have the legal authority to administer oaths? We are dealing with a matter that touches on national interest.

He added that the Supreme Court did not have the power to accept and act on the evidence the lower court did not have and act on.

Okoro wondered why Atiku sought to tender fresh evidence when the grounds of his appeal had nothing to do with forgery against the President.

Hear him:

The jurisdiction of this court is donated by the Constitution. One wonders what the appellant (Atiku) intends to do when none of his grounds of appeal is hinged on forgery against the second respondent (Tinubu). The attempt to introduce the fresh evidence is aimed at reversing the gains made in the speedy adjudication of electoral disputes that had been marred by prolonged hearings.

Matter closed! Door shut! Of course, the panel went ahead to destroy the other legs of the petition just like the PEPT did. It held INEC could not be held liable for not transmitting results electronically; that the demand for the mandatory 25 per cent in the FCT was strange and untenable; that the petitioners ought to have led evidence of electoral frauds in all the wards complained of – remember that there are 176,846 polling units in Nigeria – among other pronouncements.

Outrage? Despondency? Dejection? Nigerians, many of them, were simply benumbed. As was in the case when, for instance, Buhari won his election in 2015, when the streets went wild with jubilation, it was like a huge pall was thrown over the country, enveloping all manner of celebration. Even within the APC camp and among their supporters, mum were the words.

For many, it even got worse with Okoro, who was at the centre of it all, admonishing Nigerians to learn to trust the courts. *Trust the courts?!* It was like rubbing pepper on the raw wounds, like pouring petrol into a raging fire. I was one of those who protested this seeming unfeeling way of rubbing it in from the jurist. I not only protested silently, I went to town.

Like Fela, would always say – *I put my mouth for song,* to underscore the raison d'etre for his many protesting outings, I put pen to paper, or should I say, I hit my keyboard. Here is what I wrote in the *Whirlwindnews.com.ng* of October 30, 2023, entitled: *Pray! What manner of trust does Justice Inyang Okoro and his Supreme Court want?*

My take:

Justice Iyang Okoro made a very remarkable statement on Thursday. At the end of his judgement, while leading the seven-man panel of the Supreme Court which ended the legal challenge to President Bola Ahmed Tinubu as winner of the February 25, 2023, presidential election as announced by the Independent National Electoral Commission (INEC) on March 1, 2023, he said the public must learn to trust the courts.

Of course, the erudite jurist ought to be stating the obvious. Courts are temples of justice or have been described as such. Therefore, anyone and everyone that comes to them must bow to their authority. This of course is predicated on the assumption that judges, lawyers, and other judicial officers themselves are the priests and servants at its altar. In this wise, the pronouncements of judges therefrom are supposed to be words coming directly from God. That ought to be the source and essence of the respect and nothing more.

It is like the Pope speaking ex-cathedra – when he mounts the Papal Chair of Saint Peter to make a pronouncement – the Catholic Church believes that therein lies the infallibility of the Pope – where everything issuing from his mouth in that condition is authentic and correct teaching of the church and of God to wit.

*No true priests of Osun or Amadioha would decree the trust of the people. Their conducts and outcomes of their divinations simply speak for them. In law, it is the doctrine or dictum of **res ipsa loquitur** – the facts speak for themselves or what in internet technology is referred to as garbage in, garbage out. In other words, you cannot plant orange and demand to reap cassava. There are so many ways to put it.*

The moment it is suspected or discovered that the judgements from the courts are no longer reflective of the pristine qualities of a temple, a natural reaction follows. It is either the trust and respect they are supposed to convoke or invoke become shaky at best or at the worst, they collapse completely and, in that case, suffer the fate of the biblical salt that loses its taste and only fit for the fire as its final destination.

Is that not what is obvious in the situation at hand? To what extent have the pronouncements of the courts Okoro wants Nigerians to trust been reflective of the voice of God that dwells in the temple of justice? That is the question that he must first answer, without which his disenchantment at the reaction of the public goes into no issue. It is akin to eating his cake and having it or blaming the victim and not the oppressor, or as it is said in Nigeria, beating a child and saying it should not cry.

It is a common saying that anything that acts in the manner of a rat would naturally attract the attention of the cat. That obviously is the case here. Over the years, the Nigerian courts have acted in manners that not only raised the suspicion of the public towards their true intendments but reached outcomes that have dealt heavy blows to their impetus as the eyes and ears of God in the temple of justice.

It is a common dictum in law and many judges have also adumbrated so, that justice must not only be done but seen to have been done. To make the concept more reflective and understandable, Justice Chukwudifu Oputa JSC, as he then was, popularly referred to as the Nigerian Socrates on the bench, even expanded it to mean justice to the accused, justice to the accuser, and justice to the society.

To what extent has this been reflected in the judgements of the courts in recent years to enable them to command the trust Okoro demanded of Nigerians? Consider the case in question *regarding the Supreme Court itself. Could the apex court say with its full chest that it did not act as a rat that should attract the attention of the cats within the Nigerian society?*

This particular Supreme Court panel, which Justice Okoro presided over, holds the record today for posting the fastest judgement time in the history of Nigeria. At no time had the apex court given such a critical judgement in such a record time. Three days to prepare and read a judgement in a presidential election is such an extraordinary feat to say the least.

Ordinarily, that particular speed ought to earn the panel and the judges a special mention on the pages of honour for being so diligent to their call, especially in view of the dictum that justice delayed is justice denied. Yet did it? Was that the case? Certainly not! Why? The answer simply lies in the sequence of events that occurred before it. Many did not see the urgency that would lead to the speed in the face of the prevailing circumstances, especially with the information preceding it.

The reason is simple. Outside the main substance of the presidential election and its outcome, a bigger issue had come up in its wake – the true identity of President Tinubu, a development whose implications clearly outshone the other questions about the credibility of the election itself during the pendency of the matter.

Before then, Atiku Abubakar, former Vice President, as the presidential candidate of the PDP, had roused the interest of not only Nigerians but indeed the entire world with the damning issue of the depositions at the District Court of Illinois, Chicago in the US regarding the Chicago State University (CSU) where the President claimed to have obtained the degree certificates he submitted to

INEC.

At the time the admissibility of the matter was being argued at the apex court, there was another argument at a court in the US where Atiku was again pressing the judges to order the US Federal Bureau of Investigation (FBI) to release its much-touted dossier on Tinubu, which he and his supporters believed would have given a further impetus to their claims that the President was complicit in all manners of crimes, including identity theft, which would make him unfit for the number one job of Nigeria he presently occupies.

It was a few hours after the District Court in Detroit reportedly denied the former VP the request to release the record before the October ending in order to aid the Supreme Court to decide on what to do, that Okoro and his panel decided to move. Therein lay the suspicion! Who could actually blame anyone that believes that they were working to an answer, even if the intentions of their lordships at the SC were noble?

Three days to prepare and deliver a judgement was incredible in Nigeria simpliciter! It even got curiouser with the pronouncements of the Okoro panel proper. Who told Okoro and his men that what Nigerians and indeed the world were looking for were to hear their mastery of the law as was showcased during that judgement on Thursday? No! Nigerians and the world were looking out for answers to clear questions.

Who won the 2023 presidential election in Nigeria? If you agree with INEC that it is Tinubu, how? All Atiku, Peter Obi, his counterpart at the Labour Party, their supporters, and indeed a groundswell of the public wanted was a glean into the real and entire contents of the Independent Results Viewing (IReV) Portal of INEC that showed the images of women in the bathrooms or eagles chasing their preys.

They also wanted a credible judicial scrutiny of the contents of the Bimodal Voter Accreditation System (BVAS) which Atiku and Obi actually got from INEC itself after such a tortuous process so as to ascertain and to prove to Nigerians that Tinubu truly won the election. Did their lordships provide the answers as required of them? Were they supposed to, and if yes, what response were they expecting if they did not? In other words, having provided what the public needed in the breach rather than substance, how then do they want to get the trust?

Today the critical questions trailing Tinubu's true identity remain in the public domain – in the back-and-forth ding-dong of speculation – no thanks to the reticence of the courts to settle it finally. Even before, the likes of Yinka Odumakin, a member of the inner circle of Tinubu's empire, affirmed that his real name is Yekini Amoda Ogunlere from Iragbiji in Osun State, many of his close associates had cried out and pointed in that direction like a crying baby would point in the direction of the mother.

Coming back from the US court, Atiku et al had equally pointed in the same direction in the allegation that Tinubu's depositions on oath to the INEC as required by law are untrue as the certificate he presented from the CSU was forged. But instead of delving into the matter to affirm the veracity of the document or denounce it, Nigerians were offered loads and loads of law. In the end, like the Gordian knot, Tinubu's identity remains a mystery.

Yet Okoro demands the trust of the people? From where will it come? Trust is neither hawked in Balogun or Dugbe markets nor is it a common commodity like the fura the Fulani woman sells at Kaduna Central Market nor the okpa the Nkanu women carry around on their heads at Ogbete Market in Enugu. Trust comes from integrity and integrity comes from demonstrable evidence of constructive human behaviours over time. It is not forced; it is earned!

This was the essence of Justice Musa Muhammad Dattijo, JSC made on Friday during his valedictory speech to mark his retirement from the apex court when he told his colleagues: "My lords, distinguished invitees, ladies and gentlemen, it is obvious that the judiciary I am exiting from is far from the one I voluntarily joined and desired to serve and be identified with. The institution has become something else." Nobody could have put it better. And surely, his indictment was a tip of the iceberg.

Olisa Agbakoba (SAN) did a follow-up on Monday when he added, after endorsing all the former SCJ described the apex court as toxic, stressing the dictatorship tendency at its leadership.

Hear him:

"Out of the three arms of government – the executive, the legislature, and the judicature, the most undemocratic is actually the judiciary. The huge amount that is budgeted for the judiciary is not reflecting in the welfare of the judges because there is a mafia there. I know of judges who have passed on as a matter of critical illnesses. On the budget, we have to have a democratic process whereby the funding is spread and not just retained.

Do you know that when a Supreme Court judge retires, he leaves his house to nowhere. The only person who gets a house in the Supreme Court is actually the CJN. He has a choice of two houses, one in Abuja and probably one in his home state.

And sometimes this runs into billions. So that is part of why the situation in the Supreme Court has become so toxic."

So, if Okoro et al. and those before him who took a similar route in deciding on such critical matters were content in skirting around the issues by dishing out trailer-loads of law in place of answering simple questions, they might as well hold on to their law while the people hold on to their trust. They could decree Tinubu as President of Nigeria. They have the power to do so as they have demonstrated. What they do not have the power to do is command public trust. That is left to Nigerians to give – to those deserving of it! Chikena! Yes! Those were my words and I still own them today as I did then.

But I was not alone. The media buzzed with similar opinions. Jubril Samuel Oketepa (SAN), after the Supreme Court verdict, warned that Nigeria's democracy was on its way to the mortuary. Appearing as a guest on *Prime Time*, a public affairs programme on Arise News Television on November 23, 2023, he stressed his position thus:

It is an unfortunate situation that the judiciary, that is the arm of government that has been given the onerous responsibility of stabilising democracy, appears to have created more roadblocks for those who lost elections to prove the allegations in the petition.

I must commend parliament that following the outcries of Nigerians that election petitions are hard to prove, parliament introduced section 137 of the Electoral Act to say that where there is obvious non-compliance in the face of the document, then you can look at the document and make pronouncements. But the insistence of some of our courts that you must call witnesses, including polling units by polling units' agents of political parties, for me has put a spanner in the growth and development of democracy in Nigeria.

I have written that if our judiciary can take judicial notice of who goes to the television stations and who addressed the press after court proceedings and are angry or upset as a result over the conduct, they must also in the same vein take judicial notice of the conduct of politicians. For instance, how many political parties do we have in Nigeria? They are more than 18. Now you're expecting that agents have carbonised copies of result sheets. How legible are those carbonised sheets?

Now parliament in their wisdom says we're going to use BVAS machines and once elections are conducted at the polling units, the BVAS machine is used to scan and then uploaded on the IReV. Then we came to our judiciary who we trusted would now hold INEC accountable and responsible for the innovations introduced in its own manual that BVAS becomes sacrosanct to determine the integrity and credibility of elections for the courts to say that BVAS plays no significant role until you've gone through all the processes and that you could manually collate results; for me, those decisions have taken Nigeria's democracy from the 21st century to the 13th century or stone age where we no longer recognise the importance of technology.

I was in the legal team of Peter Obi and in that legal team we were able, for instance, to get certified true copies of over 18,000 blurred images uploaded on IReV. They were subpoenas that were issued on INEC for the documents to be produced. INEC did not produce the documents. At a point in time, it got to a point that an institution that was in disobedience to a series of court orders — mark you, subpoenas are orders of the court — institu-

tions that were not respecting court orders got a pat on the back by no single sentence either in the Court of Appeal or in the Supreme Court condemning that attitude.

Indeed, the referee became more of an attack in the field of litigation than even those who were recruited to engage in the attack. There were a series of objections coming from INEC which ought not to be. Then you come to the argument that you must frontload a subpoenaed witness statement along with the petition; I do not think that is possible. Are we saying that if I plead for a document from INEC, I must now get a court order to front load INEC statement? Who will sign it? Will INEC staff sign it?

So there were a lot of complications and roadblocks put in the way of petitioners. Not only did it make it difficult and an uphill task, but it also made it impossible. It was impossible because the document that we needed to have – indeed you may recall that even the demand for payments of CTC (Certified True Copy) of documents became so outrageous. We reported it. But the decision of the court is the decision of the court.

INEC is not independent. How can it be? There is no independent institution in Nigeria in practical reality. Anybody who tells you that INEC is independent, that is a story you can tell to infants in Tales by the Moonlight. In practical reality, no! Because there are some things that happen that shouldn't happen for an institution that is independent. When we talk about institutions that are independent, not in Nigeria, because there is no loyalty to the Federal Republic of Nigeria by those who have the responsibility to give loyalty to Nigeria.

The loyalty is to either those in power or to those who have the capacity to dictate the tune of what you're supposed to do, popu-

larly regarded in Nigeria now as the cabal. There are cabals in our electoral jurisprudence; there are cabals in so many of our institutions that they have no respect for what is called democracy. Because democracy in Nigeria is not a product of the sovereignty of the people. If it were so, we would not have what we are having. INEC, and when I say INEC, I mean some of the staff, not all, and only an infinitesimal number of them – because the chairman of INEC now, for instance, cannot be everywhere in the polling units – who did you recruit to go to the polling units for purposes of conducting elections? Did they obey the rules and regulations churned out by INEC? Are we holding them accountable?

On Thursday, August 8, 2024, Okutepa, was on song again, this time as the guest speaker at the first Inter-Party Advisory Council Roundtable on *The Role of the Judiciary in Nigeria's Democratic Sustainability,* held in Abuja. In a captivating treatise, the erudite lawyer, was no less lacerating of the judiciary, concluding:

True democracy is far from Nigeria. The news making rounds in our elections since the advent of civilian rule in most cases are worrisome and frightening to say the least.

Substantial justice, which is actual and concrete justice, is justice personified. It is secreted in the elbows of cordial and fair jurisprudence with a human face and understanding. Technical justice, in reality, is not justice but a caricature of it.

This time, he had company in Sam Amadi, a Harvard-trained lawyer and economist. The former Chairman of the National Electricity Regulatory Commission (NERC), currently law teacher at the Baze University, Abuja, while delivering one of the most robust, profound and scholarly dissection of the issues, in a speech punctuated by thunderous applause, told the audience that the

Nigerian malaise could be captured not in the abundance of brilliant people, but paucity of sincerity and honesty.

"There are so many brilliant people, but there few sincere and honest people, Amadi, is also an alumnus of the Kennedy School of Public Policy, outside picking a doctorate degree in law from the prestigious US institution, while commending Okutepa, regretted that while in other climes, electoral outcomes were the functions of messaging and mapping of strategies, the Nigerian variant was centred on corruption.

I serve you the full doze:

In every country, elections are won on strategies. So, in the US today, you see policy people thinking around messaging, thinking around mapping constituencies. In Nigeria as well, election is won on strategy. And the strategy of election in Nigeria is very simple – bribe INEC, bribe the judiciary, commandeer the security and you're done.

The people that destroyed the 2023 elections are INEC and judiciary. The rules were clear. The electoral act is not perfect; I'm surprised that any judge, who understands administrative law, which I have taught in the university for years and which I studied under the best in the world, would argue that an internal regulation built on a law - an act, directing that you will do X, you can choose to do Y, when there is a legitimate expectation and a detrimental reliance.

INEC was totally wrong and the Supreme Court got it all wrong. And the courts – Supreme Court, downwards, got it wrong. When an agency created under the law, with an enabling act, and the constitution that says you can make rules, makes rules, those rules are laws. They can unmake it through rule-making process.

If they don't, they are bound to obey it.

"Results should have been transmitted electronically. I'm ashamed – I have a PhD in law and I can stand anywhere in the world to face the best and brightest – I'm ashamed that the courts affirmed that INEC could just walk away from the law.

For five years, I was a regulator of electricity. When we make rules, it is the same way INEC makes rules, we made those laws – tariffs – they are legal instruments, they are binding laws. I hold INEC responsible and I hold the courts responsible for the failure of the elections.

It is important to clarify who can sue. Electoral jurisprudence – the problem with Nigeria's elections is that they don't electoral jurisprudence. Electoral jurisprudence is that the court's job is to restore back power to the people voting in democracy. The problem is not between Mr. Amadi and Mr. Okutepa. It is about the peoples' right to elect their leaders. Therefore, we shouldn't be saying that only those who contested and who could have won, should file electoral petitions.

No! citizens, who voted, have a right to go to court and say that the process was faulty. Look at the US elections. All the cases that went to court in 2020, were mostly by civil society groups and voters. That should change. Now, what does take to nullify elections. I always wonder what judges call substantial compliance. If elections are conducted outside the rules, that is enough to nullify the election. You don't have to prove that you would have won. Elections should be nullified if they are conducted contrary to rules. Our jurisprudence is faulty on that.

Too much burden on judges is caused by INEC. I make this clear. The new electoral law provides two safeties that were destroyed.

First – Internal Democracy – it says that all candidates must be elected directly or indirectly. If you choose indirect, then it lays down democratically elected.

Let me say it clear, the court has the right and the duty to over-rule parties if they present candidates they didn't go through their rules or the constitution of their own internal rules. Members of the party have a right to due process and that's why the act provides for it, why the constitution provides for it. If you do not second-guess politicians, then, it doesn't mean you're imposing candidates, you're requiring them to follow their rules. That's what the Supreme Court has been saying before.

INEC needs to start doing administrative adjudication. Every process in an election, including rule-making, including declaring results, are administrative procedures that require due process. INEC should be sitting and making rulings on objections during collation of results. I watched the drama, where INEC says, call results, you call results and INEC says, go to court. No, that's not the way. There is an intermediate procedure before adjudication in courts – that is administrative hearing. You must establish the validity of those results through a process that INEC can now make rules, which the courts can now review.

Politicians are mad dogs. You need to police them. But when the policer of the mad dog is himself mad, then, that is confusion. The judiciary should no longer be thinking about politicians as people who want to do public good. The public interest is to impose order and regularity in politics and not to allow politicians to self-regulate. That is a lesson of history.

I don't blame politicians, I blame the judiciary, I blame INEC, because they abandoned their work and the politicians are the ones who can never see power and leave power. You have to treat them as persons who have adverse interest to public interest and force through regulation the convergence of private and public interest.

For those yet to connect the dots, the revelation made by one Adamu Bulkachuwa – the senator who represented Bauchi North in the Ninth Assembly, offered a further inroad into the massive rot in the judiciary. Called up to speak at the valedictory session of the Ninth Senate, the former diplomat had practically dropped a bomb in the red chambers.

He had told his audience of how he personally influenced his wife, Zainab Bulkachuwa, the first female President of the Court of Appeal, to influence the cases of his friends and colleagues, including those in the Senate with him. Before the beaming klieg lights and rolling camera tapes, he had tried spilling the beans.

He began:

Particularly my wife, whose freedom and independence I encroached upon while she was in office. And she has been very tolerant and accepted my encroachment and extended her help to my colleagues... But before he could advance further Lawan, with hot sweat breaking suddenly on his forehead, despite the air conditioner in the Senate Chambers, cut in sharply, stopping him in his track saying: Distinguished, I don't think this is a good idea going this direction.

But enough damage was already done. Even in those few words, the Senator had said enough. What was left out could easily be pieced together. Not that Nigerians were not aware of the revelation he made at that session. His comments only went further to re-emphasise what was already in the public domain.

To add to the drama, Rochas Okorocha presented his own perspectives to underscore the perfidious situations by resurrecting the case of Akpabio and Lawan. Turning to Lawan, he said:

I did not contest for Senate this period. I only contested for the office of the president. You are a very smart politician. How you came back [to the Senate] is another chapter in our political history that we need to discuss. I was there in the field with you, running for President, I never knew how you were able to meander, leaving some of us. Next time, you must teach me how to do that.

Lawan, in reply, merely retorted:

It was easy. I was there with you in the field and after our defeat, my constituents thought they needed me again. They asked for me to come back and it was a tortuous journey because we had to go through the courts. I didn't even appeal the judgement that did not give me the contest. The party and the stakeholders appealed on my behalf up to the Supreme Court so there is nothing critical or remarkable. In fact, you have nothing to learn from it.

But Okorocha, former Governor of Imo State and senator who represented the Senate at that time, appeared unfazed by what he must have interpreted as an attempt of the exiting Senate president to be clever by half when he riposted:

I want to be your student next time. It is more of the more you look, the less you see.

Of course, Nigerians who watched the melodrama understood the subject matter quite clearly. They also knew between the two who the joke was on. Okorocha himself was one of the candidates in the APC primaries. He knew that he could not go back and contest for the Senate because the law barred him from doing so. In other words, the puerile explanation of Lawan did not cut any ice. Neither did it with Nigerians.

In essence, Oketepa had his arguments cut out for him. Outside the Akpabio-Lawan saga, he could have chosen scores of other cases. So, nobody would be at sea when warning the judiciary that they might be the first target to any uprising arising from the anger of Nigerians, the erudite lawyer added:

Justice is rooted in confidence. When right-thinking members of the society go away saying that justice has been compromised, then that society is heading to a calamitous end. The way we're going – go to any of the political parties, begin with their primaries – it is imposition. And instead of those of us who have the responsibility in the department that has been exclusively reserved for the legal profession to hold this political class accountable, we seem to have allowed ourselves to be cowed. The greatest asset to darkness is light. And we are the light. The legal profession represents light.

But it appears to me that there is darkness in Nigeria – gross darkness! And that gross darkness appears to even have overshadowed the light of the legal profession so much so now that people are debating judgements of their lordships. People are debating the character of lawyers. The reasons are obvious – there are no consequences to behaviours.

In Nigeria today, you can see a lawyer advocating that you are a woman but by tomorrow the same lawyer will turn to argue that you are a man. In other civilised countries when you engage in such cameleonistic jurisprudential advocacy, you're punished. What we're doing in Nigeria is the rule of convenience and not the rule of law. That is why law in Nigeria knows who is big and who is not big. Justice ought to be blind but it appears to me that in some cases not only that justice sees, it sees those it needs to see.

But, if anyone still harboured a shred of doubt about the veracity of Okutepa's damning dissection of the parlous situation, Justice Muhammad Dattijo expanded it even more poignantly from an insider's context. Yes! Okutepa's pejorative view was one in the millions of pungent, lacerating commentaries. Yes! A ground-swell of Nigerians could not just fathom the obvious contradictions arising from the long-established dictum of the courtrooms as the temple of justice recklessness with which the supposed ministers have bespattered the same temple with the paintbrush of shame.

But it was Musa Dattijo Muhammad, until October 27, 2023, Justice of the Supreme Court, second most senior of the apex court and deputy chairman of the NJC, next to the CJN, who presented what appears one of the most incisive, clear, and authoritative perspectives to the subject, particularly coming from the angle of an insider. Mounting the rostrum on that day during a valedictory speech, with which he bowed out of the bench and officially ended a 47-year-long career, he clearly endorsed the abiding feeling out in the public that the Nigerian judiciary is oozing the stench of corruption, sleaze, and mismanagement, all completely self-inflicted.

Nobody could have missed the words from the accomplished jurist, the message they conveyed, and the pain with which he delivered them. Nobody could have missed the impact as well. Everything was there, not only in his spoken words but his facial expression and body language, even though he appeared to have laboured to choose his words carefully, as many years of practice and experience must have taught him. He actually began by telling his audience that his first choice was to quietly walk away to his home after his exit with his discontent bottled up but had to succumb to the pressure from family and friends to empty them before he left.

Hear him:

I had wanted to leave quietly on attaining 70 years, from which age our Constitution prescribes a judicial officer shall cease to be one. Why then the subsequent reconsideration and the fact of today's event? This is indeed a pertinent and legitimate question to ask. It was my view that valedictory sessions only provide honorees the platforms to tell their stories and informed by experience in the course of service make suggestions as to how to improve the institutions they had served. I was however unable to appreciate the extent to which previous suggestions had been exploited to effect the desired reforms. Members of my family and close friends prevailed upon me to reconsider my position. They insisted that it is defeatist to allow failure in utilizing suggestions proffered at previous occasions to deter subsequent contributions.

The quest for institutional improvement, particularly in the judiciary, they insisted, must rather be intensified to avoid hastening the demise of our society. A society they significantly reasoned rots too easily when institutional defects are ignored. I capitulated and thus the unfolding event today. He was then to ask the abiding question while providing the answer at the same time thus: *"Now how has the Judiciary fared in the course of my journey? The journey was calm and fulfilling until about halfway through my Supreme Court years when the punctuating turbulent cracks made it awry and askew.*

Yet he was not done! Part of the curious picture in the handling of the presidential election petition was the absence of judges from certain zones in the country, particularly the South East. No Igbo man sat on the panel both at the PEPT and the Supreme Court. Dittijo, said it was not only deliberate, but dangerous.

Hear him again:

"When I exit today, the North Central zone that I represent ceases to have any representation until such time new appointments are made. My lord Hon. Justice Ejembi Eko, JSC, who also represented the zone, retired on the 23rd of May 2022. It has been a year and five months now. There has not been any replacement. With the passing of my lord Hon. Justice Chima Centus Nweze, JSC, on 29th July 2023, the South East no longer has any presence at the Supreme Court. My lord Hon. Justice Sylvester Nwali Ngwuta, JSC, died on 7th March 2021. There has not been any appointment in his stead for the South East. To ensure justice and transparency in presidential appeals from the lower court, all geo-political zones are required to participate in the hearing. It is therefore danger-ous for democracy and equity for two entire regions to be left out in the decisions that will affect the generality of Nigerians. This is not what our laws envisage. Although it can be posited that no one expected the sudden passing of Hon. Justice Nweze, JSC, yet it has been two years and seven months since the previous Justice from the South East died, and no appointment was made.

Ditto for the replacement of Justice Eko, JSC, of North Central who exited nearly two years ago. Hon. Justice Sidi Bage, JSC, now his Royal Highness the Emir of Lafia from the North Central, had earlier voluntarily retired. He equally is yet to be replaced. Also, it was clear ab-initio that I would be leaving the court this day on attaining the statutory age of 70. It is then not in doubt that there has been sufficient time for suitable replacements to have been appointed. This is yet to occur. When on the 6th of November 2020, the Supreme Court, for the first time in its history, got a full complement of 21 justices with the swearing-in of eight justices, little did anyone know that we were only a few steps to unimaginable retrogression. As it stands, only four geo-political regions- the South-west, South-South, North-West, and North-East are represented in the Supreme Court. While the South-South and North-East have two serving justices, the North-West and South-West are fully represented with three each. Appropriate steps could have been taken since to fill outstanding vacancies in the apex court. Why have these steps not been timeously taken? It is evident that the decision not to fill the vacancies in the court is deliberate. It is all about the absolute powers vested in the office of the Chief Justice of Nigeria and the responsible exercise of the same.

Need any more be said? What the erudite JSC, did not mention was that even at the PEPT, no judge from the South East featured as well. Was that an omission of deliberate as well?

But Dattijo did not stop there. Not only did he dwell on the official sleaze in the handling of judiciary funds, he pointed to how judges now publicly and privately hobnob with bad companies unheard of before and delved into the texture of the appointments proper even when they were made where "children, spouses, and mistresses" of serving and retired judges and managers of judicial offices "are appointed in place of more competent Nigerians" all of which he contended wreaked corruption.

Hear him:

A couple of years ago, appointment to the bench was strictly on merit. *Sound knowledge of the law, integrity, honour, and hard work distinguished those who were elevated. Lobbying was unheard of. I never lobbied, not at any stage of my career to secure any appointment or elevation. As much as possible, the most qualified men and women were appointed. That can no longer be said about appointments to the bench. The judiciary must be uniquely above board. Appointments should not be polluted by political, selfish, and sectional interests. The place of merit, it must be urged, cannot be over-emphasised. Encapsulating the public discontent and even contempt for the judiciary, he traced how they came about all but dressing them in the wig and gown flowing from the activities of unscrupulous judicial officers who, instead of resisting the lure of social influences, interference from outside forces and no less official intimidation, had succumbed to them.*

Hear him again:

Public perceptions of the judiciary have over the years become witheringly scornful and monstrously critical. It has been in the public space that court officials and judges are easily bribed by litigants to obviate delays and or obtain favourable judgments... A number of respected senior members of the bar, inter alia citing Ahmed Lawan, the former President of the Senate, and the Imo Governorship appeals, claim that decisions of even the apex court have become unpredictable. It is difficult to understand how and where by these decisions the judicial pendulum swings. It was not so before, they contend. In some quarters, the view is strongly held that filth and intrigues characterize the institution these days! Judges are said to be comfortable in companies they never would have kept in the past. It is being insinuated that some judicial officers even campaign for the politicians. It cannot be more damning! President Muhammadu Buhari in 2016 ordered the forceful entry into the houses and the arrest of justices, some of whom were serving at the apex court. Not done, in 2019, the government accosted, arrested, and arraigned the incumbent Chief Justice before the Code of Conduct Tribunal for alleged underhand conduct. With his retirement apparently negotiated, he was eventually let off the hook. In 2022, a letter signed by all the other justices of the Supreme Court, including the current Chief Justice, the aggrieved protested against the shabby treatment meted to them by the head of court and the Chief Registrar. At the centre of the friction was their welfare and the cavalier attitude of the Chief Registrar thereto. In the event, his lordship Ibrahim Tanko Muhammad disengaged ostensibly on grounds of ill-health.

In all, Dattijo, staring into the thousand eyes focusing on him at the huge hall including that of the CJN, his colleagues at the apex court and other officials of the law in and outside public and private as well as members of the public, delivered a damning verdict: *My lords, distinguished invitees, ladies and gentlemen, it is obvious that the judiciary I am exiting from is far from the one I voluntarily joined and desired to serve and be identified with. The institution has become something else!* What else needs be said?

VESTED INTERESTS: THE DESTRUCTIVE MONSTER!

On August 18, 2013, Sanusi Lamido Sanusi, then Governor of the Central Bank of Nigeria (CBN), spoke to a group of young Nigerians in Abuja under the banner of *TEDx Youth*, a grassroots initiative that encourages young people to harvest, grow, and nurture new ideas. I must have listened to that lecture more than a thousand times, and each time I do, it brings to the fore the stark nakedness of the Nigerian question.

I don't know anyone that had dealt with the issue in such an authentic, eloquent, and scholarly manner as the former CBN boss, now the 16th Emir of Kano. The way he dissected the issues could only accentuate the fact – that the real problem of Nigeria is like an object in the palm of the hand that does not need any mirror to observe.

Entitled: *Overcoming the Fears of Vested Interest*, Sanusi first established the historical trajectory of Nigeria's economic growth – how the country, which in 1960 was the preferred investment destination, preferred to Japan, has remained at the bottomless pit of economic retardation despite its potential as a result of this debilitating factor.

Regretting that Nigeria had continued to dwell on only mere talks about its potentials while countries like China, Malaysia, Indonesia, Japan, Korea, and Vietnam, previously behind, had turned their own potentials into reality, he sees vested interest as a the ugly hand as the barrier the country must break.

I serve you the entire dish:

In four years in Abuja, I have come to the conclusion that we need to overcome the fear of vested interests. I will talk you through a little bit of my own experiences as governor of the central bank and use that as a basis or as a template for what I think we need to do to change this country.

I became governor of the Central Bank of Nigeria in 2009 and this was in the middle of the global financial crisis. I came to the central bank knowing that banks have problems and believing that the crises were caused by global crises – by the collapse in the capital market, the collapse in the price of oil, and that they will be fixed by addressing the normal risk management issues in banks.

Shortly after I came in and we went into investigations, I discovered that the Nigerian banking system was infested with the same corruption of the rentier system in this country; that a number of the banking chief executives had taken their banks and fleeced those banks and literally taken away depositors' money to buy properties all over the world. And like people do in ministries, in government agencies and whenever they have opportunities in oil companies, the banks were themselves a site for rent-seeking.

The fundamental character of the Nigerian state is that for decades, since we found oil, it had existed not to serve the people but as a site for rent-extraction by a small minority that controls political power. And it doesn't matter where this group comes from – whether it is North or South or Muslim or Christian or Military or Civilian – the state had always been a site for the extraction of rent with the exception of a few years that we can think of when we had development. And this is at the heart of the problems of this country.

Now, when we discovered this, and I'll give you an example because these are well-known now – they've been published – you know, there was one chief executive officer that took away from her bank over N200 billion. That is over a billion dollars. And where was this money taken to? Purchase of properties. We recovered from one CEO 200 pieces of real estate in Dubai – real estate in Johannesburg, real estate in Potomac in Washington apart from shares in over 100 companies. And all of that was purchased with depositors' funds.

We went to court in the UK on the case of another CEO, we got a judgement on that CEO for N142 billion – stolen from the bank – taken to go and buy shares and manipulate the shares of his own institution and also transferred outside to purchase properties. Now, the first CEO we were able to convict. We recovered these assets and got a six-month sentence and sorted it out.

The second CEO, we finished our case, established in Nigeria – we had a criminal case in the UK, we had a criminal case in Nigeria – established the case – two weeks before the final statements were made, the judge was miraculously promoted to the Federal Court of Appeal – after three years of trial – at the very end of trial – because someone – a very popular religious leader with hundreds of thousands of supporters carried him to political authorities and the system that was supposed to protect us and handle criminals was used and manipulated to promote a judge so that he would not convict a thief.

Now, this is an example and an instance of the kinds of things that happen in the country that stops the country from reaching its full potential. But my experience in the banking reforms and how it affects the fear of vested interests were the following:

After we discovered the things that happened in the banks, the critical thing we had to do was to take a decision that would pitch us against powerful political and economic forces. We were dealing with chief executives that in 2009 had become invincible. They were in the seat of power. They had economic power and they had bought political protection. They were into political parties; they had financed the election of officers, and they believed that nobody could touch them.

Every time I said it was time to take action, people said to me, you can't touch these people, you will be sacked. You can't touch these people, they'll kill you. You can't touch these people. But I said, you know what? We're going to take them on. And we took the decision that we're going to remove them. And you know what, we removed them and nothing happened; we're going to prosecute them and we're going to put them in jail and put one of them in jail; and we're going to recover these assets.

Because the way the central bank operated in the past was that these guys take all this money and the central bank says the bank has failed. The bank that we saved had N4.4 trillion in deposits. They had 8-10 million customers. But the government had always bet on the side of the rich people. Because these customers, the old woman in Gboko or Yenagoa or in Maiduguri who had been told to save her money and who had saved money for 40-50 years and all her money are gone.

The civil servant who had worked for 35 years kept his money in the banks, the school fees, the medical bills, wakes up one day and he finds that his bank is barricaded because his bank has failed. Banks do not fail. When people say banks have failed it's like seeing a man whose throat has been slit and you say the man died. He did not die, he was killed. And those who had killed the banks, those that destroyed these deposits had always walked away. They become Senators, they become governors, they become captains of industry. And they set up new banks and they continue and for millions of poor people who don't have a voice, that's it.

Nobody knows the number of Nigerians who have died from failed banks because they were sick and could no longer pay their medical bills because the money was locked up in a bank that has failed. Nobody knows the number of children whose parents could afford to pay their school fees who had to drop out of school because the banks had failed.

So, we used this as one instance, as one example of what we can do if we wanted to confront these vested interests and deal with them for the first time. But the banking industry is just one part of Nigeria. What is happening in other areas?

Take the oil industry.

We talk about fuel subsidy. In 2009, this country paid N291 billion as subsidy for petroleum products. By 2011, this number had jumped to N2.7 trillion. Did we start consuming 10 times as much petrol? Did we have 10 times as many cars? Did the population of Nigeria multiply 10 times? I did not believe those numbers. I screamed against those numbers, a number of people screamed, and of course we tried to remove subsidy and there was Occupy

Nigeria (protest).

There had been investigations and what did we discover? That a lot of that money never went to fuel subsidies that were consumed by Nigerians. There were people in this country that produced pieces of paper and brought to the PPRA and somebody stamped those pieces of papers and said that they brought in petroleum products and paid them subsidy. Those pieces of paper said I brought 30,000 metric tonnes on so and so ship and we discovered that that ship was nowhere near the coast of Nigeria on that date. We had seen vessels that did not exist or were retired on bills of lading and money had been paid. And you know what, as I speak to you, none of them has gone to jail.

This is the only country in the world where you have something called oil theft where vessels come and take crude oil and literally drive out of the country. You see the numbers every day – 100,000, 200,000, 400,000 barrels a day. Nobody even knows – N7.3 billion! How does anybody take oil in a vessel and leave the country?

We've got the Navy, we've got NIMASA, we've got security services, we've got oil companies themselves and every day we complain about development. We don't have development because vested interests continue to rape and take the money out. The only way you're going to move from potential to reality is to stop preaching and start asking yourself how can we overcome the fear of vested interests and how can we confront them.

And if there is one thing I learnt from banking it is that they are not to be feared. They stand on quicksand. They've got only two toes, they're not too intelligent, it doesn't take too much intelligence to steal, if they were smart, they probably would not be stealing, they'll find other things to do. They have two weapons and two weapons only. First is how much do you want? And if you don't want anything then I'm going to destroy you.

If you don't want their money and if you're not afraid of them you destroy them. There's nothing in there. You're more intelligent. And we've to ask ourselves as a country, how have we allowed ourselves to be reduced to a level that is so far below our potential?

A few weeks ago, I was in Lagos at Tinubu's birthday at the colloquium where I spoke to young people. I said we have 65 million youths in Nigeria, what does it take for one of you to get the votes and become the president of Nigeria? What does it take to say you're tired of my generation, we're going to get one 40-year-old, intelligent, committed, patriotic Nigerian and we're going to get all the youths to vote for him? What does it take to address this problem sector by sector? Identify these interests one by one and confront them? Why does it have to take fuel subsidy removal for us to come out and challenge the rot that is in our country? What are we afraid of?

We're afraid of losing the security that we have today. We may not lose it today, we'll lose it tomorrow. So there is one message I have for every Nigerian is to remember that the problems of this country are enormous but the solution is simple. And that solution is that we must overcome, we must recognise that at the heart of the problem of Nigeria – at the heart of 90 per cent of our issues from Boko Haram to religious ethnic crisis, to religious crisis, to lack of employment and to the heart of healthcare is that there are people who profit from the poverty and underdevelopment of this country. And these people are called – Vested Interests!

So long as they remain entrenched, so long as we have not over-come the fear of them and dislodge them, we are not going to find the solution to these problems and we're not going to reach our full potential.

Of course, Ngozi Okonjo-Iweala in her book – *Fighting Corruption is Dangerous* was no less pungent in dishing out perspectives to enhance Sanusi's very vibrant and well-informed submissions, warning about the same dangers inherent in confronting this monster.

One element Sanusi seemed to have left out, however, is that Vested Interest is not just a local phenomenon. It has an inter-national dimension which is several times more intriguing, more compelling, more powerful, and more dangerous than the local forces that are involved.

Femi Falana (SAN), Nigeria's foremost rights activists had made allusions to an aspect of it when he appeared as one of the speakers at *Felabration*, a yearly event to celebrate the late Af-robeat king, Fela Anikulapo Kuti in 2021, where he argued that the Western nations, which stigmatise Africans with the tag of corruption, are far worse culprits.

Hear his argument:

Yes, Africans are corrupt but do not be tempted to jump to the conclusion of the West that stigmatise us as the most corrupt on earth. It's not true. America, Britain are the most corrupt coun-tries on earth. Transparency International tries to rank corrupt countries. They say Nigeria is corrupt, Ghana is corrupt, Camer-oon is corrupt, but Switzerland, which warehouses all the corrupt money in the world is never in that reckoning.

My own addition to Falana's position had to do with a later development. In 2014, Goodluck Jonathan had approached the US to buy weapons to fight insurgents then ravaging the North East. That was after the abduction of the Chibok Girls. The deafening din that trailed that ugly event must have alerted him that his office was in danger, hence his desperation to contain the problem. But the US, ostensibly peeved with him for signing the anti-gay marriage Act just passed by the National Assembly into law, refused to play ball.

Desperate to get the arms willy-nilly, he had tried the backdoor channel to procure them from the black market. However, on September 15, news broke of how a private jet belonging to Ayo Oritsejafor, a Nigerian pastor and then President of the Christian Association of Nigeria (CAN), stashed with about $10 million cash was arrested in South Africa.

It turned out that the plane was actually on that secret mission to procure those arms? Much as it may appear ordinary faux pas to the ordinary eyes, discerning minds easily made the connection. Who squealed on that mission? Of course, many eyes focused in one direction with the concluding answer – those that refused to sell the arms legally.

Then came the next set of questions. How did they know? If they could trace the operation of that highly secret mission that must have been plotted at the highest level of government, is it not the natural conclusion that they ought to be aware also of the sources as well as movement of the same arms into the hands of those dark souls using it to cause mayhem in and across African countries? Why are they not being stopped in the same manner they stopped the mission sanctioned by the Nigerian government?

If anyone was in doubt about this, Jonathan himself was to clear it when he dumped the blame for his inability to return for the second term at the feet of Barack Obama, former US President, confirming the heavy backing of Washington for the emergence of Buhari as President notwithstanding his uninviting anti-democratic records as a brutal military ruler.

Hear him:

I can recall that President Obama sent his Secretary of State to Nigeria, a sovereign nation, to protest the rescheduling of the election. John Kerry arrived in Nigeria on Sunday, January 25, 2015, and said 'it's imperative that these elections happen on time as scheduled.'

How can the US Secretary of State know what is more important for Nigeria than Nigeria's own government? How could they have expected us to conduct elections when Boko Haram controlled part of the North East and were killing and maiming Nigerians? Not even the assurance of the sanctity of the May 29, 2015, handover date could calm them down.

Of course, anyone who knows the former president and his propensity for circumspection might suspect that he did not spill the entire beans to his audience on that 20th November 2018 during the launch of his book *My Transition Hours* in Abuja. He might not have revealed the private discussion he had with the top envoy or his boss, which might include subtle and open threats. Who would dare an Obama after he supervised the events that led to the brutal killing of Muammar Gaddafi, the Libyan President, through NATO forces he led?

By the time the Nigerian president was being confronted by Kerry and Obama, the stains of Gaddafi's blood would still be visible at the spot where he was killed in Sirte on October 20, 2011. Was it surprising that he had to become the first African president to throw in the towel when the results of his election were still being counted in 2015? Figure it out.

Could these developed countries truly deny that they are not aware of the security crises ravaging African countries? Many people will swear that they do. Reason! Where will all the weapons from their factories go if everywhere is calm and quiet? So, call them conspiracy theorists. But they have convincing arguments to make that these insurgencies are sponsored by the West for several reasons – to entrench their political and economic interests.

Sponsored to keep their arms factories booming, to create a flourishing economy back home, to extract mineral resources from territories seized by sponsored bandits, or to ensure that brothers are pitted in arms struggles against each other for the same purpose. They cite examples of Libya, a thriving nation that was deliberately destabilised for this purpose. Of course, many other examples follow – South Sudan, Nigeria, the Sahel Region of Africa, among others.

In fact, driven further, not a few would swear that these countries are actually living in mortal fear of the day the African continent will not only be stable but will enjoy good leadership because that will end the penchant for their leaders carting away loads of cash, which they either salt away in bank vaults in these foreign lands or sinking them in purchasing choice properties. That will also be the end to illicit exploitation of their natural resources through various means including sponsorship of insurgency or outright stealing like is happening with the Nigerian oil.

Indeed, Peter Obi's political ordeal is linked to this phenomenon. It is believed to be the major factor that dealt a heavy blow to his mandate. The international elements and local collaborators ensured that he never got to power. Why? Obi's presidency would have dismantled their well-established structures found in every facet of the Nigerian polity. He would have gone all out for the vested interests as he did in Anambra as governor, where he not only fought against a similar group that held the state down by its throat, but defeated them. Though Chris Ngige, his predecessor started the battle, Obi finished it up in his silent, unobtrusive way, without throwing a punch and without the cataclysmic eruption of violence that symbolised the Ngige era.

It is therefore given that he must have sent jitters to similar camps of buccaneers and syndicate operating in Nigeria by his pronouncements. They must have looked into their crystal balls and discovered that the LP boss, was not dishing out empty words, but had the intention and gusto to carry his threat through. They knew he meant business when he told the world that he was going to eradicate the crude oil theft and check the corruption in the subsidy regime.

In one of his interviews, he made it clear that crude oil was being stolen by the same government crying out against the crime. His reasoning is that oil was not like a piece of chewing gum or a wrap of sweet someone could steal from the shelf and hide in his pocket, stressing that no ship could enter Nigeria's territorial waters without the knowledge of Nigerian authorities, let alone lift crude. Therefore, to him, all those who ought to guide the Nigerian territorial waters were not only complicit but culprits. Of course, it was not only Nigerians that heard him, the cabal also did. So, while the people gave him the mandate to do the job, these powerful oil bandits across the globe, in collaboration local agents did what they had to do. They stopped the mandate. Who would have imagined what went on in their camp as they reviewed the implication of an Obi presidency? Panic! That would have been an understatement.

Yes! Obi, may have declared that he would remove subsidy on Premium Motor Spirit (PMS). But was that all he said about it? No! He first described it as a scam. What if he really had the magic wand to plug the loopholes as he did in Anambra as governor? Would there have been any need to travel that route in the end? Even if he did, would the result under his supervision be as devastating as what Nigerians have been experiencing since that May 29, 2023 declaration by Tinubu?

Now, Obi right from the outset had started shouting about the indiscriminate borrowing. His voice croaked as he warned when the government, like a drunken sailor, squandered all they borrowed only to return to NASS for approval to borrow more. All his protestations were met with mockery and taunting from the same government as well as their supporters. Yet the creditors, who were aware that these funds returned back to their countries through corruption-induced back-channels or ended in private pockets, were all more eager to lend more. Would they want an African leader that would change that paradigm? Never! It suited them perfectly that corrupt politicians or their agents would steal the entire money and bring it back to them by other means, directly or indirectly.

So, an Obi was a clear certainly a bad deal. He even capped it all, when he changed the music with his own mantra – from consumption to production – with details of the steps to he would take to attain the goal. What if this comes through? They must have survived heart attacks or cardiac arrest at the prospect of the entire wastelands in the North being turned into a massive agricultural belt instead of a breeding ground for insurgents and bandits. They must have weighed the implication of Nigeria no longer available as a dumping ground for their goods.

Yes! It could be politics and they had heard it before. But what if? What if this "crazy man" suddenly stops the importation of petroleum products by not only fixing the refineries but creating grounds for building new ones? What if he blocks all the loopholes for pillaging the commonwealth as he threatened and stayed the thieving hands in Nigerian and beyond? What if this man fixes Nigeria? What if Nigeria recovers? What if Nigeria works?

No! The risk is so great. Nigeria working would certainly have a domino effect. What if other African countries, drawn like bees to the nectar, copied the model and fixed their own countries? Who would want to risk a new world order in which Africa would be independent economies and no longer the hewers of wood and drawers of water?

The answer to all these troubling assessments of the unravelling situation, and the prospect of a New Nigeria, was what resonated in that singular act of the shutdown of the IReV and rendering the BVAS useless on the morning of February 25, 2023? Discerning Nigerians are therefore not fooled with the ignoble story of a glitch INEC gave as the reason for the failure of the device. It could only be the capitulation to the evil hands of VI who wanted the status quo to remain for them to continue to run riot and roughshod over the polity. They have since succeeded.

Like Okutepa said, Nigeria has since returned to the stone-age electoral model. It began with the March 18 governorship and state assembly's election that followed where this time the electronic devices seemed to have played no roles at all. The November 11 governorship elections in Kogi, Imo, and Bayelsa have since cleared all doubts about how deeper the process has since sunk.

But who could have put it better than Chimamanda Ngozi Adichie, globally renowned novelist, storyteller, and activist, who in her letter to US President Joe Biden complaining about the endorsement of the election by the US State Department opened all the pores to spill everything there was to spill including the hypocrisy of Uncle Sam and their collaborators in Europe?

Again, I serve you that epistle entitled *Nigeria's Hollow Democracy* in full:

Something remarkable happened on the morning of February 25, the day of the Nigerian presidential election. Many Nigerians went out to vote, holding in their hearts a new sense of trust. Cautious trust, but still trust. Since the end of military rule in 1999, Nigerians have had little confidence in elections. To vote in a presidential election was to brace yourself for the inevitable aftermath: fraud.

Elections would be rigged because elections were always rigged; the question was how badly. Sometimes voting felt like an inconsequential gesture as predetermined "winners" were announced.

A law passed last year, the 2022 Electoral Act changed everything. It gave legal backing to the electronic accreditation of voters and the electronic transmission of results in a process determined by the Independent National Electoral Commission. The chair of the commission, Professor Mahmood Yakubu, assured Nigerians that votes would be counted in the presence of voters and recorded in a result sheet and that a photo of the signed sheet would immediately be uploaded to a secure server. When rumors circulated about the commission not keeping its word, Yakubu firmly rebutted them.

In a speech at Chatham House in London (a favourite influence-burnishing haunt of Nigerian politicians), he reiterated that the public would be able to view "polling-unit results as soon as they are finalised on election day."

Nigerians applauded him. If results were uploaded right after voting was concluded, then the ruling party, the All Progressives Congress, which has been in power since 2015, would have no opportunity for manipulation. Technology would redeem Nigerian democracy. Results would no longer feature more votes than voters. Nigerians would no longer have their leaders chosen for them. Elections would finally capture the true voice of the people. And so trust and hope were born.

By the evening of February 25, 2023, that trust had dissipated. Election workers had arrived hours late or without basic election materials. There were reports of violence, of a shooting at a polling unit, and of political operatives stealing or destroying ballot boxes. Some law-enforcement officers seemed to have colluded in voter intimidation; in Lagos, a policeman stood idly by as an APC spokesperson threatened members of a particular ethnic group who he believed would vote for the opposition.

Most egregious of all, the electoral commission reneged on its assurance to Nigerians. The presidential results were not uploaded in real-time. Voters, understandably suspicious, reacted; videos from polling stations show voters shouting that results be uploaded right away. Many took cellphone photos of the result sheets. Curiously, many polling units were able to upload the re-sults of the House and Senate elections but not the presidential election. A relative who voted in Lagos told me "We refused to leave the polling unit until the INEC staff uploaded the presiden-tial result.

The poor guy kept trying and kept getting an 'error' message. There was no network problem. I had internet on my phone. My bank app was working. The Senate and House results were easily uploaded. So why couldn't the presidential results be uploaded on the same system?"

Some electoral workers in polling units claimed that they could not upload results because they didn't have a password, an ex-cuse that voters understood to be subterfuge. By the end of the day, it had become obvious that something was terribly amiss.

No one was surprised when by the morning of the 26th, social media became flooded with evidence of irregularities. Result sheets were now slowly being uploaded on the INEC portal and could be viewed by the public. Voters compared their cell phone photos with the uploaded photos and saw alterations: numbers crossed out and rewritten; some originally written in black ink had been rewritten in blue, some blunderingly whited-out with Tipp-Ex. The election had been not only rigged but done in such a shoddy, shabby manner that it insulted the intelligence of Nige-rians.

Nigerian democracy had long been a two-party structure—power alternating between the APC and the PDP—until this year, when the Labour Party, led by Peter Obi, became a third force. Obi was different; he seemed honest and accessible, and his vision of anti-

corruption and self-sufficiency gave rise to a movement of supporters who called themselves "Obi-dients."

Unusually large, enthusiastic crowds turned up for his rallies. The APC considered him an upstart who could not win because his small party lacked traditional structures. It is ironic that many images of altered result sheets showed votes overwhelmingly being transferred from the Labour Party to the APC.

As vote counting began at INEC, representatives of different political parties—except for the APC—protested. The results being counted, they said, did not reflect what they had documented at the polling units. There were too many discrepancies.

"There is no point progressing in error, Mr. Chairman. We are racing to nowhere," one party spokesperson said to Yakubu. "Let us get it right before we proceed with the collation." But the INEC chair, opaque-faced and lordly, refused. The counting continued swiftly until at 4:10am on March 1, the ruling party's candidate, Bola Tinubu, was announced as president-elect.

A subterranean silence reigned across the country. Few people celebrated. Many Nigerians were in shock. "Why," my young cousin asked me, "did INEC not do what it said it would do?"

It seemed truly perplexing that in the context of a closely contested election in a low-trust society, the electoral commission would ignore so many glaring red flags in its rush to announce a winner. (It had the power to pause vote counting to investigate irregularities—as it would do in the governorship elections two weeks later.)

Rage is brewing, especially among young people. The discontent, the despair, the tension in the air have not been this palpable in years.

*How surprising then to see the US State Department congratu-
late Tinubu on March 1. "We understand that many Nigerians
and some of the parties have expressed frustration about the
manner in which the process was conducted and the shortcomings of technical elements that were used for the first time in a
presidential election cycle," the spokesperson said.*

*And yet the process was described as a "competitive election "
that "represents a new period for Nigerian politics and democracy."*

*American intelligence surely cannot be so inept. A little home-
work and they would know what is manifestly obvious to me
and so many others: The process was imperilled not by technical
shortcomings but by deliberate manipulation.*

*An editorial in The Washington Post echoed the State Department
in intent, if not in affect. In an oddly infantilising tone, as though
intended to mollify the simpleminded, we are told that "officials
have asserted that technical glitches, not sabotage, were the issue," that "much good" came from the Nigerian elections, which
are worth celebrating because among other things "no one has
blocked highways as happened in Brazil after Jair Bolsonaro lost
his reelection bid." We are also told that "it is encouraging first
that the losing candidates are pursuing their claims through the
courts," though any casual observer of Nigerian politics would
know that courts are the usual recourse after any election.*

*The editorial has the imaginative poverty so characteristic of
international coverage of African issues—no reading of the country's mood, no nuance or texture. But its intellectual laziness,
unusual in such a rigorous newspaper, is astonishing. Since when*

does a respected paper unequivocally ascribe to benign malfunction something that may very well be malignant—just because government officials say so? There is a kind of cordial condescension in both the State Department's and The Washington Post's responses to the election. That the bar for what is acceptable has been so lowered can only be read as contempt. I hope, President Biden, that you do not personally share this cordial condescension. You have spoken of the importance of a "global community for democracy" and the need to stand up for "justice and the rule of law." A global community for democracy cannot thrive in the face of apathy from its most powerful member. Why would the United States, which prioritizes the rule of law, endorse a president-elect who has emerged from an unlawful process?

Compromised is a ubiquitous word in Nigeria's political landscape—it is used to mean "bribed" but also "corrupted" more generally. "They have been compromised," Nigerians will say to explain so much that is wrong, from infrastructure failures to unpaid pensions. Many believe that the INEC chair has been "compromised," but there is no evidence of the astronomical US-dollar amounts he is rumoured to have received from the president-elect. The extremely wealthy Tinubu is himself known to be an enthusiastic participant in the art of "compromising"; some Nigerians call him a "drug baron" because in 1993 he forfeited to the United States government $460,000 of his income that a Chicago court determined to be proceeds from heroin trafficking. Tinubu has strongly denied all charges of corruption. I hope it will not surprise you, President Biden, if I argue that the American response to the Nigerian election also bears the faint taint of that word compromised because it is so removed from the actual situation in Nigeria as to be disingenuous. Has the United States once again decided that what matters in Africa is not democracy but stability? (Perhaps you could tell British Prime Minister Rishi Sunak, who quickly congratulated Tinubu, that an illegitimate government in a country full of frustrated young people does not portend stability.) Or is it about that ever-effulgent nemesis China, as so much of U.S. foreign policy now invariably seems to be? The battle for influence in Africa will not be won by supporting the same undemocratic processes for which China is criticized. This Nigerian election was supposed to be different and the U.S. response cannot—must not—be business as usual. The Nigerian youth, long politically quiescent, have awoken. About 70 percent of Nigerians are under 30, and many voted for the first time in this election. Nigerian politicians exhibit a stupefying ability to tell barefaced lies, so to participate in political life has long required a suspension of conscience. But young people have had enough. They want transparency and truth; they want basic necessities, minimal corruption, competent political leaders, and an environment that can foster their generation's potential. This election is also about the continent. Nigeria is a symbolic crucible of Africa's future, and a transparent election will rouse millions of other young Africans who are watching and who long too for the substance and not the hollow form of democracy. If people have confidence in the democratic process, it engenders hope, and nothing is more essential to the human spirit than hope. Today, election results are still being uploaded on the INEC server. Bizarrely, many contradict the results announced by INEC. The opposition parties are challenging the election in court. But there is reason to worry about whether they will get a fair ruling. INEC has not fully complied with court orders to release election materials. The credibility of the Nigerian Supreme Court has been strained by its recent judgments in political cases, or so-called judicial coronations, such as one in which the court declared the *winner of the election for governor of Imo State a candidate who had come in fourth place. Lawlessness has consequences. Every day, Nigerians are coming out into the streets to protest the election. APC, uneasy about its soiled "victory," is sounding shrill and desperate, as though still in campaign mode. It has accused the opposition party of treason, an unintelligent smear easily disproved but disquieting nonetheless because false accusations are often used to justify malicious state actions. I supported Peter Obi, the Labour Party candidate, and hoped he would win as polls predicted, but I was prepared to accept any result because we had been assured that technology would guard the sanctity of votes. The smouldering disillusionment felt by many Nigerians is not so much because their candidate did not win as because the election, they had dared to trust was in the end so unacceptably and unforgivably flawed. Congratulating its outcome, President Biden tarnishes America's self-proclaimed commitment to democracy. Please do not give the sheen of legitimacy to an illegitimate process. The United States should be what it says it is.*

Sincerely,

Chimamanda Adichie

What else could anyone add? Just as she wrote, the action of Washington was quite deliberate. Apart from the verdict of international organisations like the European Union, which correctly highlighted the fraud in the electoral process, agents of the US in Abuja and those working underground through various channels must have filed their individual reports that would tell the accurate story clearly. That story would be that Peter Obi won the election. But their prompt endorsement of the flawed election is probably because Obi did not fit their bill as an African president. How could an African president not be open to greedy acquisition of wealth? Why should an African president not be amenable to owning private estates in Western countries? Not even a mansion in Potomac or some fancy beach resort in Miami? They must have run a check and had a full dossier that would confirm Obi's claim that he had just one residential house in Onitsha and no other place. They must have ascertained that his children had no mansions of their own and were in fact ordinary struggling working employees. In fact, they would have discovered that Obi's only daughter with her multiple degrees obtained in prestigious schools in England was just a secondary school teacher in Nigeria. Surely that is not an African president that would serve the US interest. How could an African leader not have a single smear of corruption around him? How could a Nigerian governor, instead of being arrested for corruption after his stint in office, be surrounded by the trumpeting sound of how he banked a surplus of up to N75 billion? It means there is nothing to lure him with, nothing to rope him in with, and nothing to blackmail him in the West. Such a man would be independent – too independent to demand a space for his country in the global economic prosperity. Such a man could wake the sleeping giant – Nigeria. That would be dangerous – too dangerous to the US interest to be allowed. So? So!

In the end what Sanusi advocated in his treatise as the panacea to overcome VI came to pass in 2023. For the first time in Nigeria, youths across the country shunned primordial sentiments of their fathers and stood behind one man – Peter Obi to challenge the status quo and change their story. But that seed that germinated through the Obidient Movement was killed before it grew – by the same forces he cried out about – the VI. I do not know whether the monarch actually got round to this reality because surprisingly he is one of the vocal Nigerian leaders who have since gone mute – keeping the public guessing on where he actually stands with regards to the heist that denied the people their choice in that historic event.

MY DECLARATION

- Peter Obi won the presidential election of February 25, 2023. Anybody that fails to acknowledge that is either ignorant or deliberately engaging in subterfuge, mischief or outright lies. WS's claim that he only *dented* or *made impact*, but did not win, falls into any of these.

- The 2023 presidential election was a political relay game between Buhari and Tinubu in fulfilment of an agreement that ended in *Emilokan* (It is my turn), the cardinal message on which the latter based his campaign. Buhari did not only play his part, he did so by breaking the law publicly. Recall that the electoral law forbade voters from exposing their choice. Buhari ignored that injunction by not only voting for Tinubu, but showing the world his choice. He dared not only Nigerians to do anything about it, but the law. That was the level of the impunity.

- Peter Obi's victory had national appeal. It was not an ethnic, sectional or regional occurrence. Indeed, from the outset, he had clearly spelt it out to Nigerians that nobody should vote for him because of where he came from and nobody should vote for him out of pity, but out of the belief that he was going to lead them to the New Nigeria of their dream. No other candidate was bold enough to make such a declaration. Nobody could have, because that was what they needed to survive. So, WS, was wrong by introducing ethnicity into the matter. The attempt to swing the narrative or tint it in ethnic colours, was indeed, a convenient, deliberate mantra, which he copied straight from the Tinubu and APC camp, as a strategy to further diminish the Obi brand. In fact, it was Tinubu, his candidate and their supporters that kept playing the ethnic card, which invariably did not work, given the way he failed woefully in Lagos, a city that he supposedly built, but which denied him at the eleventh hour.

- Peter Obi did not engage in any *Gbajue*! He did not engage in any form of intimidation, cajolement or pressure to force himself into office. There was no plot anywhere to forcefully change government or truncate democracy. The suggestion by Afe Babalola (SAN), for a transition government, was purely a statesman's wise counsel, only a sage, who fearing the worst, such as the last election, wanted to make to save his country from imminent collapse. So, WS's counter reading of this intention was a deliberate effort at misinterpretation in order to aid a flawed narrative – crying wolf where there was none.

- Some of us in the anti-Abacha movement won't have survived if not for him. When WS, made this declaration in his speech at the Tinubu colloquium in 2013, what did he mean? Was that not a vindication of the argument Sunny Igboanugo made in the article: Soyinka, Obi, Tinubu: When repayment of mafia debt is inescapable – whirlwindnews.com.ng of September 19, 2023, which gave birth to Baiting Igbophobia: The Sunny Igboanugo Thesis? I rest my case.

- Obidient Movement is not a violent group. It is an assemblage of millions of Nigerians, mainly of youth age, probably seeing the same vision of a New Nigeria in which they will not be forced to sell their inheritance to travel out of the country into life of uncertainty in foreign lands or die in the biting cold weather in Canada and other European countries as second-class citizens. So, WS's emotions is at best a reflection of transferred aggression, anger and righteous indignation that they are not following him into the ditch Nigeria is heading under his watch and encouragement of a government that is leading the way. At the age of the same youths, the selfsame WS, did worse in his passion for the country that resulted in his paying with his freedom. These youths do not wish *The Man* to *die* in them, by keeping *silent in the face of tyranny*.

Did I hear he later denied calling Patience Jonathan a Shepopotamus? It was all over the space in those days. Let me concede he didn't. But I have not heard he denied calling Jonathan, her husband Nebuchadnezzar? I don't know about you, but I would prefer the former than the *Nebu* tag. It sounds more elegant to me.

"I shall not insist that the biblical figure of Nebuchadnezzar is uniquely apt for the pivotal figure of the 'democratic' history in the making at this moment. For one thing, Nebu was a nation builder and a warrior. One could argue even more convincingly for the figure of Balthazar, his successor, or indeed Emperor Nero as reference point – you all remember him – the emperor who took to fiddling while Rome was burning." Obidients did not write this. They could not have gone this far. Soyinka not only did, but put a voice to it at a press conference in Lagos in a statement he titled: *King Nebuchadnezzar – The Reign of Impunity."* Date was December 2, 2014. Soyinka was already 80 at that time!

- WS's war with these youths did not start with Peter Obi and therefore has nothing to do with Peter Obi. Its origin could probably be traced to that infamous trip to Port Harcourt, where the Rivers State Government under the watch of Rotimi Amaechi, allegedly spent a whopping N82 Million to organize his 80th birthday on August 1, 2014. The controversy that resulted from that outing must have created the room for the Kongi to start hating the purveyors of the immense criticisms, mostly coming from the social media. Then came in 2016 when he threatened to destroy his Green Card if Donald Trump, then the Republican nominee, won that year's presidential polls. The social media society, made up of the youths took him to task when Trump eventually won and the war deepened. If WS actually destroyed the document, he did not do so publicly as he had threatened. He has since been quoted as saying that he would re-apply after the former POTUS, was convicted of sexual assault, on May 30. Therefore, the darts against Obi, is a deliberate diversion purely to promote the Tinubu and APC agenda.

- WS's recent declaration that Obi will not win the 2027 presidential election and therefore should not try is not only preposterous, but another classic example of abortion before pregnancy. The reaction from that outlandish statement must have told him that he is at worst standing alone and at best standing with a few – the Tinubu supporters and APC gang. In fact, on the contrary, Obi will win with larger numbers if he stands again in 2027. What Kongi could bet on rather is INEC – the commission will reenact the 2023 oddity and the judiciary will complete the job as usual. Obi might even be declared a distant fifth this time around, assuming he is allowed to run.

- WS, as a man of the pen should realise that there is nothing new under the sun including electoral fraud and its disputes. When the late Ikemba Nnewi, Emeka Odumegwu Ojukwu, described the late sage, Obafemi Awolowo, as *the best President Nigeria never had,* during his burial in Ikenne, Ogun State, on May 9, 1987, Nigerians knew what he was talking about. Awolowo never even bothered to return to court in 1983, when the NPN machinery rigged him out once again. His experience in 1979, was enough to stop him. There is no telling the fact that the APC would definitely repeat the 1983 "feat" of landslide victories. Hopefully, at 93, WS, will still be very much around to do a yeoman's job again.

- WS's attempt to dress Peter Obi and or Sunny Igboanugo in ethnic garb, worst of all introducing Biafra and IPOB angle into it, in his *Baiting Igbophobia: The Sunny Igboanugo Thesis,* is the most heartbreaking depiction of the sudden change of a man who had devoted more than half of his earthly life not only to nationalistic struggle, but speaking truth to power. Kongi hinges his intervention, in his INTERVENTION SERIES, on what he calls "false attribution" and "lies" contained in the piece: *Soyinka, Obi, Tinubu: When repayment of mafia debt is inescapable – whirlwindnews.com.ng* of September 19, 2023. Though he acknowledges the event under reference, he says it was actually during the NADECO struggle and not after and that he, Soyinka, wrote the letter of introduction to the Taiwan authorities and not Tinubu. Granted! But, does this obvious gaffe detract from the substance of the message of that piece? The piece, in the main, was to reflect the *paddy-paddy* nature of the Soyinka-Tinubu relationship. The detail was just an ancillary to beef it up. Was there a gaffe? Confirmed! But Kongi could have labelled the author with tag of gross incompetence and indolence. Sunny Igboanugo would have accepted the docket of a lazy and slothful journalist and left it there. Why the ethnic slur? Nothing from the beginning to the end, suggested ethnic phobia or Igbophobia, to use his words. Sunny Igboanugo, a Lagos Boy, has since been weaned of any form, shape or nuance of ethnicity, long before the amniotic fluid dried on his head.

- To underscore the fact that gaffes are as human as death itself, read this: *Mr. Peter Obi was gainfully occupied with his righteous business of trading while elections took place somewhere else. The results were annulled — via that Judicial Gesture — his party was the beneficiary and that party slotted in his name as its representative flagbearer!* This was the same WS, writing in the introductory part of *Baiting Igbophobia: The Sunny Igboanugo Thesis* - Peter Obi's name was not "slotted in." He was not only a candidate of the All Progressives Grand Alliance (APGA), in 2003, he campaigned in the field throughout the period leading to it. In fact, he had plunged himself into the political arena long before, first as a member of the PDP, where he tried his hands for the party's ticket. Thus, I take Kongi's assertion that "the party slotted in his name" as a gaffe, unless otherwise proven to be deliberate.

- Now read this: *I would have thought being lumbered from the same initials as IPOB — P.OBI — was sufficiently problematic. Obi could not have failed to encounter claims that this was not an accident. If he has, I wish to inform him, in passing, that it proved an uphill task attempting to persuade accusers otherwise. Now, with his formal benediction on the Obidients formation, I was no longer sure that I was not wasting my time.* This was WS, writing on Page 48 of *Baiting Igbophobia: The Sunny Igboanugo Thesis.* Now, sample this for a size! If anything fits into ethnic baiting or ethnic profiling, this is it. It is like the Kongi, warning Ndigbo of Sunny Igboanugo representing them as a collective because he bears the surname, Igboanugo meaning (Igbo have heard).

He wrote: *More critically however, when one marketeer of counterfeit wares implicates an entire community through name appropriation – be this of a hamlet, village, state or – it becomes necessary for one to ensure that such a community understands the implication of the lie, and are aware that a crime is being committed in its name. The choice is then left to the co-opted: to restrain or disown the aberrant member – or to endorse its product – not always an easy choice, we know, to publicly disown one's own. We only demand that a choice is made.*

A name is more than a name, it conveys more than its literal value. IGBOANUGO means, "The Igbo have heard". The implication of this is that such a name bearer is the Ear of the community and, by association, its Voice. Self-appointed? Pen for hire? A righteous indignant? Phew! At least, a thousand families bear Igboanugo in Igboland. How then would Sunny Igboanugo be speaking for Ndigbo, because he bears Igboanugo as surname? If Wole Soyinka speaks on a matter, do we take it that a Kayode Soyinka has spoken even as they bear the same surname, not to talk about roping in the entire people who bear the surname. The obvious implication of this line of thinking is that Kongi and others like him are not only engaging in ethnic baiting or ethnic profiling, but scaremongering – a futile attempt to say the least. Who can scare

Ndigbo? If it were possible, destroy the entire Igboland today that tiny, but thriving community in Ghana or Cote D'Ivoire, Malaysia or even Afghanistan will return, increase, multiply and do more exploits.

Meanwhile when would an Okechukwu or Chukwudi speak freely in Nigeria without being reminded that he is Igbo? Why should a piece of writing by a journalist be reduced to an Igbo issue when there was no shade in the entire work that suggested so? In all the interventions Soyinka, has made over the years, was he ever so labelled with his Yorubaness? How many of them bore that ethnic insignia? Sunny Igboanugo speaks as a Nigerian and shall continue to do so!

- WS, in *Baiting Igbophobia: The Sunny Igboanugo Thesis,* depicted his robust association with several Igbo leaders – the late Christopher Okigbo, his late colleague in the literary circle, Emeka Anyoku as Secretary General of the Commonwealth, Kinsley Muoghalu, et al. In fact, in Muoghalu's case, he narrated how he practically procured the sand and cement, the planks and rods to erect the platform on which he ran for the presidency of Nigeria. Indubitable! Nobody would dispute this claim. But the difference was that Muoghalu never squared up against Tinubu. In fact, there is doubt that if Obi, had contested earlier when Tinubu was not in the picture, Kongi, would have bested other Nigerian leaders as his staunchest supporter, because he possesses all the ingredients, he had advocated all his years in crusading for better Nigeria.

Indeed, were I to listen to many opposing voices, I would not have made this effort, because among the few whom I muted the idea to, not a few had advised that I shelved replying him because it would diminish the memories of the great sacrifices Kongi made for Ndigbo, including going to jail on their behalf during the Biafra effort. I insisted on a reply all the same, not to diminish those sacrifices but to put the records straight – it is not and has never been about Ndigbo.

- On page 106 of *Baiting Igbophobia: The Sunny Igboanugo Thesis,* Soyinka recalled an encounter with Prince Moham-mad Saif Al Hakim, of the Fujairah Emirate during the Annual Conference of the International Theatre Institute, in Febru-ary 2023. The event, which he said was the first to be held physically since the Covid outbreak, and which took place in the United Arab Emirate, had him as a keynote Speaker and Guest of honour, in his capacity as former President. The conversation with the Prince, had delved into the situation in Nigeria, particularly the presidential election and more particularly, Tinubu.

The conversation, he narrated, went thus:

"How are things in Nigeria?'

"Well, you know, so-so. Not the most relaxing sphere of exis-tence. But not the most turbulent."

He chuckled. "And the elections? How is Tinubu doing? 'What do you people think?"

It was unexpected, the directness, so I became cautious in my reply: "Well-e-ell, the usual mixed feelings about all the contestants. In his case, he has an additional problem of health. People find that worrisome. I also do, quite frankly.

His response was spontaneous and any serious journalist is free to fly to Fujairah and check. The prince took a good look at me as if attempting to situate me. He tapped the side of his head and said:

"Ah, but here, is that alright?"

I nodded, Yes, adding: "I haven't heard any complaint regarding that department. The contrary appears to be the case."

He nodded satisfaction, beaming: "We were in college together, in Chicago, Brilliant. We all knew him. Talked about him a lot. We were sure he would go places. Everyone admired him. We still keep in touch."

Two main elements are deductible from this encounter – confirmation that Tinubu indeed attended Chicago State University and that he was brilliant. Another deliberate effort to market Tinubu? Search me! But, if this encounter actually took place the way it is depicted, then Soyinka was truly detached from the issues during the election campaigns. For one, Tinubu's mental health was among the major issues during the period, but probably the most critical – not with the *Bala Blu, Bulaba* mantra that even children were mouthing everywhere, and not with other numerous signs of not being in control of his mental elements.

Brilliance! No doubt. For one plotting to be President of Nigeria in the way Tinubu did – I hear it was a 30-year project – a substantial dose of brilliance and intelligence is required. But brilliance for what? For what purpose, for whom and in whose interest?

Surely, Kongi is kilometres away from that popular tag – the ordinary Nigerian – to be hit by the impact of Tinubu's brilliance and intelligence as presently reflected in the streets.

I hope that he is aware that such famed intelligence birthed those three words – subsidy is gone – that impulsive declaration with which Nigeria was plunged and has remained in the bottomless abyss of hopelessness and misery since a few seconds after his inauguration as president. I also hope that Soyinka is aware that after the price of PMS shot up from N187 to first over N500 and now over N700, the subsidy has since returned. If not, he should call Wale Edun, Minister of Finance, in the same government for confirmation and details. Such intelligence! Such brilliance!

My question! Our dear Kongi, is that brilliance reflective in the decision that the first foreign borrowing after taking office, is to buy SUVs for 469 NASS members at N160 million per unit or the N1.5 million to purchase vehicles for president's wife or the N5 billion to purchase a yacht for his use or another N20 billion to build a new home for the Vice President, or N90 billion to support hajj pilgrimage at a time Nigerians are virtually being tempted to consume their own excreta?

Does it include continuing with Buhari's evil legacy of parochialism and nepotism – of excluding a section of Nigeria from the dinner table of the APC government - of handing over the lever of authority to the *Lagos Boys* – a totally clueless, mindless, selfish and irresponsible cabal – the organised syndicate, perpetrating its actions in darkness?

Are Nigerians seeing and feeling that famed gift of intelligence and brilliance in the odious narrative trailing the unilateral award of the N15 trillion coastal road. Are they found in the sudden return to the original plan of the, after demolishing part of the multi-million-dollar *Landmark Event Centre* or the numerous own goals and faux pass to which the people have been sentenced in the past one year? Pray! Do they include the sudden plunge of the Naira from N450, to the N1,500 to a dollar?

- WS has since upped the ante by his recent declaration that Peter Obi should not contest the next edition of the presidential election in 2027, because he will not win. Reason: The LP candidate is the patron of the Obidients, his mortal enemy. It is an indication that he will still toe the same path of supporting Tinubu. Discerning Nigerians already know what this means. *Ceteris paribus* – with INEC, security agencies, the courts and other institutions in the firm hands of the APC, the Kongi is merely stating the obvious. State capture in terms of elections, has never been new in Nigeria.

- But so is the hand of God. The picture is now clear that Nigerians will have to resort to those two words with which they had confronted past situations – *God dey*! With the heavy hands of the NPN in the Republic, who would have thought those who boasted of raw power and invincibility as they plotted and executed the *landslide* election victories would be swept out of power. With all the intrigues of Babangida, the jackboot and iron-fist grip of Abacha, who would have believed that Nigeria would one day breathe the air of freedom again? Was it not that evil regime that arrogantly boasted – we are not only in government, we are in power – just to rub it in? Was it not under that regime that all the five political parties he registered came together to beg the despot to shed his khaki and run under their collective ticket as civilian President? Who would have thought that the obnoxious regime of the PDP, where their officials derisively boasted that they would be in power for 60 years, which they later increased to 100, would one day, be at the receiving end of what they dished to others for 16 years – with APC displaying the worst form of that arrogance and playing God?

What an error that WS, in all his wisdom and given all he knows about Nigeria, still does not know that it does not lie in the hand of man to determine tomorrow. What a pity. But who would blame him? Already, he is getting his comeuppance from Tinubu, his man-Friday. Roads have been named after him. The National Theatre, one of Nigeria's most iconic edifices, now has his name emblazoned to it. Who knows what will follow next – both public and private?

- I am a believer of and in Nigeria. I see my fate tied to a Nigeria. I believe that God did not make Nigeria the largest enclave in Africa for nothing. I believe that it is not in vain that the land in Nigeria will be flowing with milk and honey in every corner you scratch. I have lived in, seen and tasted a Nigeria that is the envy of the rest of the world. I believe that today's rot is in keeping with the obvious fact that until a seed falls to the ground and dies, a new seed will not sprout, grow, blossom and bear fruits. Nigeria is probably at that stage right now – being driven to its death by its present leaders from where the New Nigeria will sprout, grow and blossom and bear the fruit that will feed and satisfy its citizens – nay the world.

My dream ultimately, is to see a Nigeria where the son of the butcher in Okene, will become the governor of Enugu or Anambra, the son of a palmwine tapper in Amaechi Idodo, will become the Senator representing Zamfara, where the son of a Fulani herdsman from Kano, having settled and resided in Uyo or Osogbo, runs and wins the governorship or becomes the Speaker, or the son of a Yoruba cocoa farmer from Ikare Ekiti, will control the affairs in Borno as the chief executive of the state. I know I may not be on this side of creation to witness it. That certainly, will take years and even centuries to come, by which time, my earthly bones would have become dust and this wicked generation, including its current movers and shakers would have returned to give account to their maker – in full. But I will like to see it from whatever realm I eventually retire to.

- I believe only a Peter Obi could pave the road to such a dream in present-day Nigeria. The credentials are there, unmistakably evident. However, nobody knows the mind of God. Perhaps, He could still do it in our time. But if He wills it tomorrow or in the next 100 years, He has the capacity to create another Peter Obi of the present or even better Peter Obis. Instead of Agulu in Anambra, he could come from the womb of the granddaughter of that woman presently in IDP camp in Borno. Because for God and with God, nothing is impossible. Those are my last words!

www.ingramcontent.com/pod-product-compliance
Lightning Source LLC
Chambersburg PA
CBHW021223090426
42740CB00006B/351